CHIVALRY

The Origins and History of the
Orders of Knighthood

CHIVALRY

The Origins and History of the
Orders of Knighthood

Kevin L. Gest

Ian Allan
PUBLISHING

Chivalry
Kevin L. Gest

First published 2010

ISBN 978 0 7110 3450 1

Published by Ian Allan Publishing

an imprint of Ian Allan Publishing Ltd, Hersham, Surrey KT12 4RG.
Printed in England by Ian Allan Printing Ltd, Hersham, Surrey KT12 4RG.

Visit the Ian Allan Publishing website at www.ianallanpublishing.com

Distributed in the Unites States of America and Canada by BookMasters Distribution Services.

Code 1003/x

Contents

Acknowledgements

Preparing this book has required far more wide-ranging research and enquiry than expected when I commenced the project. It has involved much travel across Britain and Europe, many hours sifting through books and documents in libraries and archives, and reading detailed accounts compiled by academics, both from modern and earlier times.

In compiling the book I have received the help and encouragement of many individuals, for which I am most grateful: my wife, who often travelled with me to be dragged around the many sites that were of interest to me; my agent, Fiona, who encouraged me to keep at it when the going was hard work.

I owe an immense debt of gratitude to the staff of many libraries and archives who helped find forgotten books, alerted me to trails of information I might never have otherwise considered, or sought other interesting material for me. Although they are many I would note just a few libraries: Wiltshire and Salisbury; Warwick; Birmingham; Maidstone; Rochester; Cambridge; City of London; Guildhall London; Library of Freemasonry, London; and the Bodleian Library, Oxford.

My thanks go to the people I met at the Order of St John in Clerkenwell, London; Burg and City Hall, St Saviour's Cathedral and the church of Our Lady, Bruges, Belgium; the cathedral and town of Aachen, Germany; St Denis' Cathedral, Paris; Salisbury Cathedral; the Temple Church, London; and the management at the Wroxall Abbey Estate.

Please note:
The world of knights, especially those Orders that exist today or continue to operate as family honours, is a very secretive and closed world, careful in the management of its affairs and the information it makes available. Gathering information was not always easy, but it was surprising how much information was available in documents

in the public domain. Needless to say, because of the eras this book covers, much of the material consulted has been out of copyright for decades, and even centuries. Nevertheless, I acknowledge that I have read much and some information that had stuck in my head has been used and not fully referenced. If, therefore, I have inadvertently compromised the copyright of others, I most earnestly apologise and request that such errors are drawn to the attention of the publishers so that they can be corrected in future editions.

Kevin L. Gest
January 2010

Section 1

The Opening

Isn't life strange? You get older, you experience more, you learn more and you forget a lot. But there are some small incidents from your early childhood that remain as fresh and detailed in your memory as if they had happened only yesterday.

Like all small boys who have embarked on the early learning curves of life, the presence of danger and the risk to life and limb did not enter our heads. We were out to play, to have a good time – a bit of fun. Of course, our mothers had instructed us that we mustn't go there, so by totally ignoring this instruction the forbidden location only made for added adventure. Anyway, we were at least a mile from home – the grown-ups couldn't keep an eye on us all the time.

Then there was the other instruction. 'Don't come home with your clothes dirty or torn, or there will be trouble.' We knew already we were going to be in trouble.

'Don't go near the river,' we were told. The words from the grown-ups came back when, in a snaking line of five boys, we ran along the grassy bank of the river, arms outstretched, mimicking the manoeuvres of aeroplanes, tipping our wings first one side and then the other, whilst imitating an effortless airborne turn. We ran until we were out of breath and then collapsed into an area of lush long grass growing on the riverbank. This was the mistake that was leading us into trouble. We were too young to realise that the long lush grass was only like that because the ground from which it grew was marshy, and as the five make-believe aircraft made crash landings into it, our clothes became damp, grass-stained and mud-smeared.

There was no going home now and claiming we had only been to the playground that was just a short walk from home. There was much talk between the small make-believe pilots about what our parents would do to us when they saw the state of our clothes. Yet the result of the crash landings into the soft grass had a beneficial side effect. It made us realise that we were beside the river and should be careful and find a way back from the water's edge.

It was then that we saw the old building.

Just back from the riverside, on a raised embankment, ran a railway line. Beside the railway, about a half mile from us, we could just see a timber sawmill and hear the whine of the circular saw blade as it sliced through once proud tree trunks, turning them into long thin planks. That, however, was of no interest to us. The old building peeped over the top of the railway and we could see the bottom of it through a tunnel, brought to our attention by a truck, laden with wooden planks, coming out from under it. We located a footpath that went towards the tunnel. The squadron of five make-believe aircraft set off yet again and in no time at all had passed under the railway and stood at what had obviously been the main entrance of the building. To the five small boys, the building seemed enormous. There was not another building to be seen anywhere near it. It stood cold and sinister like some haunted house that featured in a child's mystery story. The grounds were overgrown. A small tree grew out of the foundations. Doors were missing; there was rubble inside. There was the remnant of a rusty chain-link wire fence along one side of the land it stood on. There were several small piles of builders' materials, bricks, sand, a few planks of wood, just left sitting in the open.

Gingerly we crept in through the entrance of the building, finding ourselves in a room where, at one end, there was a large brick fireplace, so large that we could all stand in the hearth together and look up the chimney at the small diameter of sky above. On one side of the room was a large window frame ornately carved from stone, but without glass. We looked out over the railway and across the river to a fine view of Rochester Castle and the spire of the cathedral looming large behind it. Even to small boys it was obvious that if the railway hadn't been in the way this house might have stood on the side of the river. One of the boys said he'd seen photos of windows like that in books about castles, and maybe once a king or lord had lived there. Vivid fantasies raced through our young minds.

We explored as much of the building as we could, even climbing up a ladder that had been conveniently left propped against a wall as an access to another area of the building. It was fine getting up, but we had a lot of trouble getting one of the boys back down again. He didn't like the height when he looked back down from the top of the ladder. Then we discovered a big cellar underneath the house, with ceilings that went up to a point. It must have been very grand.

Exploration of the inside of the building completed, we found ourselves outside again. Ross, the boy who lived in the house next door to ours, suggested we could build castles using the pile of sand. Soon we were digging holes in the sand, trying to make little tunnels all the way through from side to the other, pushing our arms through to see if we could touch the hand of one of the other boys in the group who was tunnelling from the other side. We were having such a wonderful outing that so oblivious were we to everything around us – including the state of our clothes – we didn't notice the small truck that had stopped just along the road, and the big man in the boiler suit bearing down on us.

"Don't you boys move," a deep rasping voice of authority suddenly boomed out from nowhere. We froze in sudden panic and turned to face the direction of the voice. Then Ross piped up and explained that we weren't doing anything, honest, mister, and we all chipped in with agreement and support. The boiler suit of authority stood over us.

"Have you been in that building, playing about?" he demanded. We said we'd been inside but only to look.

"Well, don't do it again," he said. "It's very dangerous in there for children. We don't want you to get hurt. It's very, very old. We're here to mend it."

Suddenly he wasn't so threatening any more. Johnny asked if a king or lord had once lived there because he'd noticed the window.

"No," the man replied. "But hundreds of years ago a lot of knights lived there. It was their farmhouse and they farmed the local lands and raised horses. In the old days, long before the railway embankment was constructed, it stood on the banks of the River

Medway to provide a crossing point to Rochester Castle."

These knights, it seems, even had their own ferry boats. The boiler suit seemed very knowledgeable. We were most impressed. In our minds were images of knights in shining armour, galloping off across the country, banners flying, with sword and shield at the ready. We would enact such scenes as we played together in the days ahead.

"All this land around here was the Temple Farm," the man continued, "because the knights were called The Knights of the Temple. Did you see the big cellar?" he asked. We all nodded.

"According to stories we've been told, they used to store gold and jewels down there, money that was being shipped to the King of England, kings in France, or the bishops in the Church."

Ross immediately asked, with a hopeful gleam in his eye, if there was a chance some might still be there, like hidden lost treasure. Alas, it seemed not. We were then made to promise not to come back to play around at the site again, because it was dangerous and we might get badly hurt. Our reward for giving our word was to be driven home by the man in the boiler suit, being bounced around as we sat on the wooden floor in the back of the open topped builders' truck.

When I got home all I wanted to do was talk about the adventure of the morning and the knights. All my mother wanted to talk about was how my clothes got into such a state, and where all the sand had come from in my shoes and socks.

It was in the evening as we sat around the dinner table after my father had come home from work that I was able to get to the exciting bit about the knights and the old building.

"Ahhh," he said. "So you've been playing in the old Temple Manor building. It's good to know they're doing it up at last. But that's down by the river and you've been told not to go there."

I had convicted myself without thinking, but as my father didn't press his advantage or talk of punishments – they all came later – I sidestepped the issue.

"Who were the Knights of the Temple?" I asked.

"Their other name," he replied, "was the Knights Templar. They got into a lot of battles. They were like monks, really, but monks that went to battle rather than just stay at a monastery."

"Were they really famous?" I asked.

"Oh, yes," he said. "They were all over Europe. They were a very big group, almost like the Church. But they have a reputation of having been a bit of a *dodgy* bunch."

Knights that kept gold and jewels for kings. A *dodgy* bunch. At eight years of age, they swarmed through my imagination with images of glamour and daring-do. It was but a passing phase of childhood, but the Knights of the Temple didn't leave my early life so easily. Later, I went to a school called *Temple*. Our insignia was a shield, emblazoned on which was the symbol of two knights mounted on a single horse, carrying a banner – a typical representation of the Knights Templar.

Rochester Castle still stands proudly overlooking the banks of the River Medway, in Kent. Behind it, when viewed across the river, Rochester Cathedral, of which later elements of the design were influenced by the Templars, still stands tall as a wonderful example of the mason's art. The building we stumbled into as small boys is known as Temple Manor and is now a listed heritage building. It is securely fenced off to prevent unwarranted intrusion, and access is not easy to obtain for the casual observer, except on specific days and at certain times of the year when it is open to the public. Sadly its former importance has become undermined as it has been surrounded by low cost and untidy industrial buildings. The significance of the building and the knights that once owned it, together with the farmland that surrounded it, is acknowledged by the names given to roads in the industrial complex, names like Knights Road. A large residential area close by is known as Temple Farm.

Orders of Knighthood continue to exist even today. The influence that holders of such titles have on the course of our lives should not be underestimated. Whilst many people living in countries that were formally linked to Britain and its Commonwealth will have heard of the Most Noble Order of the Garter, there are probably few others that know or realise that the Roman Catholic Church has its own significant Order – the Order of St John of Jerusalem.

Temple Manor has stood for nearly a thousand years on the west bank of the River Medway, a symbol of a different age – an age when 'chivalry' implied honour, virtue, loyalty, trust, and a way of life.

Freemasonry also claims to be a champion of moral conduct and encourages a just and upright way of life. Several groups of knights feature directly in, or are associated with, the history and structure of this ancient institution. Most such associations slip by in Masonic ceremony without notice, their significance lost or unappreciated.

Through the pages of this book, I set out some of the basic facts and history surrounding the major Orders of Knighthood of Europe and those that are the most prominent in history, in the hope that their significance will be better appreciated.

Section 2

Days before the Knight

Defining Knights and Chivalry

There are many interpretations of the term 'chivalry'. From the Anglo-Saxon Dictionary it seems that the word *cniht* was the origin of the English word 'knight'. In Saxon times the 'c' would have been silent as it is today with the letter 'k' in the word 'knight'. A *cniht* was defined as a servant, and in Old English the interpretation would have been 'youth' or 'hero'. These seem entirely appropriate to our perceptions of someone being a knight in a bygone era. The word 'chivalry' is derived from the French word *cheval*, meaning 'horse' from which there is the extension to a horse rider. Knights in the Middle Ages were therefore servants who were prepared to fight on horseback for a cause, probably in support of their feudal lord or monarch. They were the cavalry of their times.

The title 'Sir' has been a highly prized addition to a name for around 1000 years, maybe even longer. The origins are unclear, but some historians and academics believe it comes from an abbreviation of the English word 'Senior', implying a most senior servant, who in medieval times would also have been referred to as a vassal.

The concept of Knightly Chivalry was based on bravery, loyalty, obedience, honesty, trust, integrity and chastity. But it went deeper. A knight would not seek to harm an unarmed man; he would do those things entrusted to him; he would respect women and children; he would be hospitable and charitable where required. All of these things were wrapped up in a code that was a mixture of conduct and honour.

Being made a knight provided a sense of achievement and means of recognition. It still does.

Education throughout the 20th century, along with the development of film, animated cartoons, television and printed mass media, have, perhaps, left most of us with an image of chivalry that conjures up visions of powerful and charismatic medieval knights, clothed in shining armour with visor pulled down, sitting astride a magnificent white charger, seeking to rescue a damsel in distress from whatever danger was about to ensnare her. Whilst much of this imagery is wide of the mark, there are, surprisingly, elements that are based on historical credence. And it all started long before the medieval period.

There is a question as to what chivalry really is or was, how it is linked to knights, why and when it started. We are given the impression that it was about virtue, honour, loyalty and a desire to achieve good over evil, against overwhelming odds. Several in-depth scholarly works on the subject were published in the last 50 years of the 20th century. All were seeking and proposing answers to those very questions, which perhaps suggests that the answer is not as straightforward as many might think. We have a word 'chivalry', and over a long period of time numerous people and organisations have invested enormous effort drawing our attention to the notion of what it is and was, as well as when it supposedly rose to prominence. Yet the image that has been created is not really a reflection of the reality. There is legend, myth, customs of the ages, and folklore, all of which with the passing of time have either enhanced the perception of knights or helped to distort the imagery. So, what constitutes fact and fiction?

Amongst the other images that have been portrayed of knights is that they obtained their titles by being dubbed by a king, that is a sword being placed on the shoulders of the intended recipient, and the king announcing, 'Arise Sir...' Where and how did this ceremony start? And where, when and how did kings derive authority to do this? Were they the only ones who had such authority or were others also able to undertake such ceremonies? This is another intriguing aspect of chivalry and knighthood where historical facts have become somewhat blurred by the passing of time.

Yet still there is the question as to who was entitled to be a knight. Could a pauper be suddenly elevated to such a position, or was it a position strictly reserved for those chosen from the nobility? And who was entitled to be part of the nobility, anyway? As we start to look at these issues one other point becomes clear: there is a big difference between monarchy, nobility, knights and chivalry.

We should also clarify another confusion that has evolved over time. Some academics refer to the era of chivalry as being in the Middle Ages, whilst others make reference to the Mediaeval Period. (The spelling of the word 'mediaeval' has recently changed to 'medieval' in many modern publications.) Actually, they are both the same. The word 'mediaeval' is derived from the Latin for 'Middle Ages'. It is a period that most academics now associate with a time interval of about 1000 years that started with the fall of the Western Roman Empire, around 450 CE, and the period known as the Christian Reformation that gathered momentum in the early 1500s CE, an era that concluded in the rise of what has become known as Protestantism.

In short, the period that most reflects the era of the knights and chivalry that we are most frequently presented with, came to the fore in the 14th century. In some circles, there are organisations that have titles and systems of honours of 'knight' as part of their make-up even today. It is possible, therefore, to break the development of knighthoods and the chivalric attitudes that are supposed to accompany them, into four distinct periods:

pre-1050 CE
> This was an era when chivalry and orders of knighthood were not clearly defined as such.

1050 CE – 1300 CE (the era of the Crusades)
> During this period several orders of knighthood were established that had strong religious connections. Academics often define the members of these orders as being akin to warrior monks. They provided the basis for the later connotations of chivalry that developed.

1300 CE – around 1600 CE (the post-Crusade period)
An era when some of the religious orders continued, some were disbanded and there was a rise in secular orders as a reward for service to a monarch or country, usually as a warrior, and used as a stepping stone to recognition of nobility.

1600 CE onwards
(the post-Renaissance period to modern times)
This is an era of transition that starts with a continuation of the system of knights being associated with warrior-type activity, becomes increasingly secular as the period of the Enlightenment gathers momentum, and eventually gives way to developments in science, industry and commercial enterprise. In many countries and societies, such concepts of knighthood and chivalry have been abandoned as anachronisms. Some are reduced to being of ceremonial significance only; a few remain, not as warriors in the old sense, but providing a political interface.

It is the period of post-Crusade European history that gives us the most frequently visited idea of chivalry. Yet we cannot look at that era in isolation because it is events that went before it which shaped it. Equally, it is the perceptions of chivalry that grew up in the post-Crusade period that influenced other developments in the concept of knighthood.

The origins of knights and the concepts of chivalry with which they are linked are in no small way connected with the historical and cultural development of Europe in the medieval era. There are times in the evolution of man's environment when a series of originally unconnected events advance in their own way, and then come together to create or enable something else to happen. Chivalry, and the association with orders of knighthood, it seems, was rather like that. It was the product of a time when a series of innovations, some having their roots in the evolution of other cultures in distant parts of the world but whose origins are lost in the mists of time, all came together to create the right circumstances for their existence. Their time had come and they left an indelible imprint on history with their passing.

The arrival of the knights and chivalry with which they are associated really dates from an era that followed the defeat of the Christian armies that participated in the Crusades, inspired by the Roman Church, of the 12th and 13th centuries. Chivalry is therefore a concept that arose around the late 13th century and endured for the following 200 years. The romance associated with that era, whether true or false, has left an impression and inspiration in the minds of succeeding generations.

In the opening paragraphs above, we note the terms 'chivalry', 'knight', 'armour', 'horse' ('charger'), and 'person in distress'. All of these elements developed separately but came together at a crucial time in history. To place the development of the concepts of knights and chivalry in an appropriate context, we must also understand two other elements: the development of aspects of European history and the evolution and spread of a monotheistic religion called Christianity. But they are not the only elements. The world, as seen through the eyes of our ancestors, had a very different character to the way we see it today.

Our 21st century world is analysed and understood through the development of scientific principles. The world of our ancestors was based on a drive for survival and therefore a reverence for the natural world that supplied food and the sustenance of life; the forces of creation that, season after season, provided that sustenance with a degree of regularity; a great fear of unknown and unseen forces that, without warning, could result in death, or cause natural disasters which could have calamitous effects on entire tribes, communities and civilisations, or deny the sustenance that sustained life. So the world and its forces became defined by a range of symbols, easy to construct and recognise. It was inevitable that some of those symbols found their way into the culture of early chivalry.

So, first, we should look at how the development of some of the elements mentioned above evolved.

The word 'knight' is derived from the French term for a mounted warrior, *chevalier*, that in turn has its origins in the French word for 'horse', *cheval*. So the *cheval*, it seems, is a good place to start.

The White Charger

The domestication of the horse as a means of transport and burden is believed to have taken place around 5000 BCE. Many of the innovations that ultimately led to the management of horses, and thereby to the medieval knights, did not have their origins in Europe at all. For that we must look further to the east, and in particular to China.

The domestication of the horse must have been an enormous endeavour. Horses and mules are fast and, in the wild, tend to travel in mobs. The process of trying to capture one in the wild would have been a daunting undertaking, and certainly not for the faint hearted. Man had not learned to ride horses, so capturing one would have to be done on foot. There must have been a long period during which the means of controlling the animal evolved, learning how to break its wild spirit such that it could be connected to a sledge or cart – a process that would have involved experiment and a gradual building of knowledge about the anatomy of the animal. Just how this process was achieved is lost in the mists of time and open entirely to speculation. Yet, by 4000 BCE, some 6000 years ago, the spirit of the horse had been harnessed, but it still had a limited use.

We can only assume that the domestication of horses, and the attempts made to harness the power in their bodies, would have been inspired by their relative speed by comparison with many other animals. Oxen have long been used as a beast of burden with a strength that enabled a single ox to pull a well-laden cart. Whilst an ox can run, it is no match for a horse at full gallop, when given its head. A method of connecting an ox to a cart was developed by about 3000 BCE, probably in China. It consisted of a simple network of flat leather straps that passed round the body of the ox and across its chest, just beneath the neck. Quite when the concept of the rigid shafts between which the animal was placed, with the shafts connected to the harness, first evolved is again unknown, but must have followed very soon after the development of the harness, or coincidental with it. Prior to that, a stretcher or sledge-type arrangement, connected to the horse by ropes, was probably used. On display in the Museum of Egyptian Antiquities in Cairo there is a chariot, complete with wooden shafts for connecting the chariot to a horse harness that is dated to around 2500 BCE. This demonstrates that the technology of the harnessing method was very well advanced by that time. No doubt the same design of harness developed for the ox was tried on horses, but if so, it is likely that it failed. The anatomies of the ox and horse are quite different. Placing a harnessing strap across the lower neck of the horse would result in the animal strangling itself if it tried to pull a heavy load. The more it pulled, the more it restricted air to its lungs. Thus the pulling power of the horse was restricted to the chariot, a relatively lightweight cart, for many centuries, whilst the pulling power of oxen was used for hauling large wagons, ploughing, turning grinding stones and waterwheels, and other heavy tasks. In many countries of the world it still is.

According to most sources of equestrian history, it was the development of the horse collar that enabled the power of the horse to be harnessed for heavy labour. The Chinese seem to have been at the fore of several developments in the harnessing of such power, for they are credited with the invention of the collar in the 4th century CE. It was an innovation that spread gradually to Europe over the next 500 years.

Also, according to equestrian historians, the way in which a horse was managed possibly started with a ring being placed through the nose of the animal. This was much the same method as had been developed for the control of bulls or oxen. It would have been logical to use such a method in the first place; a gentle pull of the nose in any one direction would soon teach the animal that it had to turn in that direction – being led by the nose. Soon it would have been discovered that there are pressure points on the nose of a horse, which if pressed will result in a reaction from the animal similar to that achieved by a ring. These pressure points, historians suggest, were used in conjunction with what today would be regarded as a bitless bridle, a noseband or hackamore. Instead of controlling the horse by pulling on sensitive areas of the mouth as a bit does, the noseband and hackamore does the same job by placing pressure on the sensitive areas of the horse's nose. Archaeologists have discovered that early forms of devices inserted into the mouth of the horse as a means of control were in use by around 4000 BCE, and metal bits from around the middle of the second millennium BCE. A mouth bit would require straps of some kind to hold it in place. Thus it seems likely that if a noseband/hackamore style device was used as an earlier control mechanism then all the basic elements of head strapping would have been in place for the evolution of the mouth bit.

So, by about 2,500 BCE, a means of controlling movement and reaction of the horse, along with harnessing and development of robust chariots, had evolved, and that evolution resulted in the creation of a form of high-speed transport. It enabled a relatively high-speed form of communications – ideal for messaging. Yet it seems that it was some centuries after the development of the harness and chariot that the man/horse relationship evolved into an ability to ride on the back of the animal and control its movement. That seems to have taken place around 1000 BCE. With this came the capability to gain access to places that were no-go areas for chariots and carts. Thus, whether harnessed to a chariot around 2500 BCE, or ridden from about 1000 BCE, the horse became an instrument of war. History has shown us that new concepts and implements of war, once developed, change the order of battle and strategies of warfare.

It was the development of the stirrup that really brought the use of the horse into its own as an instrument of war. It is known that various devices for holding or resting the rider's feet evolved around the same time as the ability to ride on the back of the horse. These devices included loops in lengths of rope that were simply hung over the body of the horse. Evidence suggests that the first devices that come close to the modern concept of the stirrup again evolved in China, around 400 CE, and were used primarily for the ease of mounting in circumstances where no other assistance was immediately available. It took a further 400-500 years before the stirrup as we have come to know it finally flourished in Europe. Firing a bow and arrow from a moving horse would not have been too difficult, but to gain the purchase needed to effectively wield a heavy sword or long spear, later to become a lance, requires the use of braced leg muscles, and without the stirrup or some other means of enabling a braced posture the use of such weapons would have been less effective. Thus the development of the stirrup enabled the deployment of effective mounted sword-wielding soldiery that we still refer to as cavalry. Such mounted warriors became the elite force of their times.

As already mentioned, well before 2500 BCE, the horse and chariot combination provided a relatively fast means of personal transport. It was also a war machine for elite soldiers of the day. In that era, and indeed until relatively recent times, armies walked or marched everywhere they needed to go. The horse and chariot would often be used to help protect the flanks of marching columns from surprise enemy attack, to catch and dispatch enemy warriors fleeing the field of battle, and no doubt do the same to would-be deserters. There are many illustrations and ancient sculptures that depict scenes where a cluster of horses and chariots were driven at high speed into the close ranks of enemy infantry with the objective of trampling high numbers of opposing men under foot and reducing their fighting force and spirit. Later we see evidence of long blades being connected to the hubs of the wheels of the chariots so that when the chariots were driven at the enemy, the blades chopped their legs off. Then there were the chariots that contained two men, one to manage and direct the movement of the horse, and the other equipped with a spear, javelin or bow and arrow, any of which could be delivered into the midst of the opposing army in high-speed skirmishes. As these kinds of tactics brought success so more and more horses and chariots were used.

Needless to say, it is highly probable that 4000-5000 years ago – the era of the Ancient Egyptian dynasties – the sight of horses pulling chariots at high speed would have been quite awe inspiring to the masses of ordinary citizens of the world. It was an epoch when, no doubt, the braking and training of horses was a highly sought after and relatively rare skill. As the importance of the horse as an instrument of war and communication grew, it was clearly a skill that would have been substantially owned and managed by the ruling elite of the day. Owning, breeding and keeping large numbers of horses would have been expensive, and only the ruling elite would have been able to afford it. They would also have had a vested interest in ensuring that those that were potentially their enemies were not as well equipped.

As the importance of horses as part of the machinery of war and communications grew, so they became premium valued products that were bred, bought and sold by those that represented the highest levels of society. And the best, biggest, most spirited and fastest horses always commanded an additional premium. The character of the horse said much about the character of the owner.

By the era of the medieval period, the mounted warriors – that elite force we have come to know as knights – needed more than one horse to sustain them in battle. Every knight required at least four. Every horse needed to be fast and strong. After all, a warrior in a full set of body armour was not a small burden to carry. Horses could be killed or maimed in battle or they might just become tired from being urged to perform their tasks. So each knight needed other fresh horses in reserve. This meant that there was a retinue of assistants that husbanded, groomed, trained and maintained the horses. Being a knight was therefore an expensive business, so they needed to be amongst the ruling elite in the prevailing society.

Shining Armour

Quite when armour evolved is again lost in the mists of time. As the concept of warfare developed it is obvious that it consisted of two components: one was to kill your opponent; the other was to protect yourself from being killed.

The shield was probably the earliest form of armour, and could have been made from wood, or even by weaving thin branches together rather like a basket. Some historians suggest that the earliest forms of armour may well have been animal skins or furs draped across the body. This is not difficult to imagine when one considers that our ancestors, with relatively primitive tools, must have found certain animal skins quite tough to cut through. This may then have led to pads made from hardened leather, some of which could be shaped to cover specific areas of the body that were vulnerable, including the making of hats for head protection. Shields too could be made from the same material. Again, this is not too difficult to understand.

As societies evolved, so too did various crafts that worked with animal skins, leaving them to dry in the sun, and using the resultant material to fashion, amongst other things, shoes and straps. Of course, much would depend on the geographical location of one's tribe or country, and what was actually available to fashion into protective devices. Some historians note that wicker and bone may have been used. The Bronze Age – originating around 3300 BCE and lasting until about 1200 BCE – may well have heralded the use of metals as a replacement for leather. It probably took at least 500 years of working with bronze before the skills of smelting and beating it into small flat sheets that could then be worked into armour had developed. Prior to about 2500 BCE, most if not the only means of protection would have been skins or leather.

Working in metals would have opened the way to replace leather with harder protection. But, just as with the development of the horse as an instrument of war, metal plate armour would have been something that only the ruling elite of a society could afford to acquire. This probably started with breast and back plates and helmets. There are excellent examples from the Greek civilisation, including helmets. Such armour would also have been heavy and not for prolonged use at any one time. A much lighter form of armour, perhaps used prior to plates made from sheets of metal, was a form of chain-mail, created by interlocking metal circles, like rings, then small metal plates linked together with leather straps or woven cloth materials. However, for the ordinary soldier, the main source of protection remained leather, well into the era of the Roman Empire.

According to historians, a form of chain-mail evolved in Europe around 200 BCE and quickly became used by the Romans, having encountered their enemies in Gaul with it, to their own disadvantage. It involved stitching dozens of small overlapping metal discs into a base of leather and was used to fashion an armoured covering of the torso, whilst strips of leather hung from the waist to just above the knees, with similar strips falling from the shoulder to help protect the upper arms. This progressively became the typical Roman soldier's armour. For the generals, though, shaped metal armour provided greater protection and either covered an area from the knees to shoulders when standing, or from the waist to the neck when mounted. Sitting astride a horse meant that it could become uncomfortable if, for example, the front and rear plates were each made from single sheets of metal. Thus the armour gradually grew in complexity, with several elements made from narrow strips of metal that were joined together with a new invention called a rivet. This enabled some plates to flex and thereby increase the comfort of the rider.

So by the latter part of the era of the Roman Empire two of the main elements that characterise a knight – the horse and the armour – came together after probably hundreds of years of evolution of each. Thus it is to the elite of the early Roman Empire that we turn to find the fledgling orders of social structure that provided a basis for the later Orders of Knighthood.

The Roman Order

By virtue that warriors mounted on horseback can be traced back to around 1000 BCE, it is not surprising that some writers attribute the early vestiges of organisations of knights to the civilisation of ancient Greece, a civilisation that began to flourish around that time. There is, however, little else by way of evidence to support such theories.

What is clear is that in every civilisation, in every system of government, including those of the world today, there has been a mechanism for rewarding those individuals that undertook some task deemed to be for the good or protection of society as a whole. Today we see honours given to military personnel in recognition of distinguished and heroic action on the battlefield, and to some such honours an annual pension may be attached as a national token of ongoing gratitude. Honours could be military or civil and again today we see honours awarded for diligence in government affairs, or for such initiatives as the creation of a product or service that provides wealth for the nation and, with it, international prestige. In times past, such awards may have been enhanced by the allocation of lands, palaces and castles, through which successive generations of a family would accumulate wealth, power and position. In return for those positions of power and influence there would be an obligation to fight directly, or provide manpower and materials, for a nation or ruler in a time of war. In a period of peace, such positions may have involved taking an active role in the governance of society.

It is against this background that we find the creation of one of the first social organisations which has traceable beginnings that could be identified as being of the basic constitution of knighthood – the Equestrian Order of ancient Rome.

Rome, we are taught, had its foundations around 750 BCE through the conquering exploits of two brothers, Romulus and Remus. Mythology implies that Romulus became the first king of Rome.

To the north of Rome was an area occupied by a people that we know as the Sabines. To populate many of the new towns and villages in the new state of Rome, tradition has it that a number of Sabine women were kidnapped and held as wives for the Romans.

This act has been passed down to us as the rape of the Sabine women, a recurring theme in various forms of art. The Sabines demanded that their young women be returned, but this was refused. Therefore armies of the two states assembled on a battlefield. According to legend, the battle never took place because the young women of Sabine origin, previously kidnapped by Rome, positioned themselves between the two armies, some with small children that were the offspring of unions with their Roman abductors. Thus they were Sabine women but mothers to Romans. This led to the two states amalgamating as one. Following this creation of the greater state of Rome, Romulus is then credited with having formed a bodyguard of some 300 warriors, selected from the most prominent families of the two former neighbouring states. Quite how mobile this bodyguard was is unknown, but it is suggested that they were mounted on horses. Romulus apparently called them *Celeres*[1], a word which gives some credence to the idea that they were mounted, as it apparently means 'swift'[2] and could relate to an additional role as military messengers, king's messengers, or messengers of state.

With the passing of Romulus, succeeding rulers of Rome enlarged the group of *Celeres*, until around 535 BCE when Tullius became the sixth king of Rome.[3] Tullius apparently ordained that to gain admission to the *Celeres* the applicant must be selected from amongst the noble families, the wealthiest and those that possessed the largest estates.[4] This new organisational structure evolved into the Equestrian Order – an Order that sat between the ruling elite, the Senators, and the Plebeians, or ordinary Roman citizenry. With the passing of time, those of the Order who had shown courage in some military venture, or other conduct that warranted an acclamation of merit, received promotion to the Senate and thereby became accepted as members of the nobility of Rome. Elevated to this position they were therefore members of the ruling elite. Elias Ashmole, who in the late 1600s undertook extensive research into the origins of knighthood, wrote of the Equestrian Order:

'It was a constitution, as old as Tiberius's reign, that none should be admitted unless free-born, or a gentleman for three generations; and indeed, for a long time none were elected knights but the best sort of gentleman, and persons of extraction...'[5]

Like all the great institutions of past civilisations, it seems that the Equestrian Order then fell into a period of decline as the structure of Roman society changed. Ashmole goes on to note:

'Yet at length, thro' corruption of times, Plebeians and Freedmen being too frequently received into this degree... occasioned their power to grow less and less, 'till it shrunk to nothing; so that the Palaces and Offices of Judges which they before had executed, became conferrable on the Publicans. And when Cicero was Consul... the Equestrian Order stood in need of re-establishment, whereupon they were incorporated into the Commonwealth in the third degree, all acts passing in The Name of the Senate, the People of Rome, and the Equestrian Order.'[6]

He adds:

'As a mark of eminence, they had the titles of 'Splendid' and 'Illustrius' bestowed upon them, and sometimes have been called 'most Sacred' Knights.'[7]

Then, in the 5th and 6th centuries CE, the mighty economic and military Western Empire of Rome collapsed, to be replaced by a new form of Roman Empire based on religion.

The growth of a dominant monotheistic European religion
Many of the Orders of Knighthood that evolved in Europe in the Middle Ages did so in support of the Christian religion as it had been promulgated and reinforced by the Catholic Church for around 1000 years.

In 1945, a poor farmer in the Holy Land discovered a buried

earthenware jar. It contained a series of bound parchments that had lain untouched for nearly 2000 years. The contents of the jar have gradually been translated and are now referred to as the Gnostic Gospels, the Nag Hammadi scrolls. There are many archaeologists and theological scholars that consider these to be gospels that were left out of the New Testament when its form was being created. Chief amongst these scrolls is one known as the Gospel of Mary Magdalene which, again, many academics believe may have been the original text of what became the Gospel of John. These texts, and others found a few years later and known as the Dead Sea Scrolls, have produced controversial theories that challenge the orthodoxy of the religious doctrine that has underpinned western society for over 1500 years.

Although in today's culture these relatively new discoveries may have increasing relevance, in the world of yesteryear they were not known and the peoples of those eras could only react to what they were instructed to believe. Thus, by the first decade of the 21st century new information puts old ideas into a different context and has changed some of the old themes, so that when looking at the development of the Christian religion it seems more appropriate to reflect on some of the latest theories and facts, rather than those that were the mainstay but a few decades ago.

Two thousand years ago the city of Jerusalem was part of an extensive territorial area which was, at that time, occupied by and administered as part of the Roman Empire. A man by the name of Yehoshua[8] was, we are told, put to death by crucifixion. Quite what he had done that should have so ensured the wrath of the Roman authorities is not quite clear. There are those who claim he was a prophet, distributing the word of the deity. There are others who believe he was a priest, an anointed leader of his community, who had lived in a devout enclave known as the Essenes, at Qumran, just outside Jerusalem – a community whose beliefs were a strict form of religion and culture derived from the Hebrew faith; that he taught tolerance and built up a strong following amongst the poorer people of Judaea, such that the ruling hierarchy of the Jerusalem temple, who derived power and authority from Roman rule, found their positions threatened. There are still others that suggest he was seen as the promised messiah[9] (king), the Son of God, who came to Jerusalem to liberate the Jewish population from Roman enslavement and that his mission was to lay the basis of a revolt against Roman rule.

Whatever the truth, the punishment of crucifixion was largely reserved for those who the authorities of the time perceived as being guilty of inciting insurrection against their rule, which suggests that they viewed his activities as being a threat or direct challenge to Roman authority and the stability of part of their empire. Around 30 years after the crucifixion of Yehoshua, a major insurrection against Roman rule did take place. It resulted in the Herodian Hebrew Temple, built on the former site of Solomon's Temple in Jerusalem, being utterly destroyed by the Roman army. It had been the third such temple built by the Jews on the same site. Such a temple would never rise again. The final victory of the Romans occurred in 70 CE, with the capture of the last stronghold of Jewish rebellion, at Masada.

The name Yehoshua is more widely known to us as Jesus. It is a Latin word derived from the Hebrew and Greek equivalents of Jesu, Jeshua, Joshua, Yehoshua.[10] The word 'Christ' apparently signifies a person that was suitably anointed to assume the authority of a leader, a tribal ruler or king.[11]

The exploits of Yehoshua were recorded by scribes who, we have been taught, were named Matthew, Mark, Luke, John and Paul – Paul having been previously known by the name Saul. With the crucifixion of Yehoshua, it is believed that James the Lesser, sometimes also known as James the Just and believed to have been a brother of Yehoshua, became the first bishop of the revised faith known as the Church of Jerusalem. Tradition has it that James was later murdered by the Sadducees and Pharisees of the Herodian Temple for preaching that Christians need not undergo circumcision or observe the ceremonial attributes of the Laws of Moses. This outraged the hierarchy of the Temple in Jerusalem and the fate of James was sealed. Thus it was that Peter, the apostle, formerly a fisherman and known by his real name of Simon, became the head of the new faith. Paul, it seems, set out on missionary journeys that saw him visit many of the major eastern Mediterranean cities of that era, passing on details of the deeds undertaken by Yehoshua. Peter also undertook missionary journeys, taking a different route from that of Paul. Peter's route culminated in his arrival in Rome around 42 CE. Here, according to tradition, he spent the next 25 years, using the city as a base for his own missionary undertakings.[12] Also according to tradition, the Crucifixion took place around 33 CE, in which case, if Peter did arrive in Rome in 42 CE, it was a mere nine years after Yehoshua's death.

Both Peter and Paul had their lives terminated in Rome in 67 CE during the Neronian persecution of the Christians. History tells us that Nero, Emperor of Rome from 54-67 CE, was responsible for starting a great fire that raged for more than six days and destroyed most of the residential area of the city. It started in an area of small streets and crowded wooden buildings through which the fire quickly took hold, killing thousands of the residents. In the subsequent inquiry into the cause of the fire, informers were bribed to claim that it had been started by Christians. Thus, whilst Nero set about designing a new city, which he proclaimed should have the name Neronia as a memorial to his architectural achievement, Christians became the subject of persecution, torture and death. It was during this period of persecution that both Peter and Paul were killed. The Catholic Encyclopedia describes Peter's death as follows:

> *'Concerning the manner of Peter's death, we possess a tradition...*
> *that he suffered crucifixion. Origen says: 'Peter was crucified at*
> *Rome with his head downwards, as he himself had desired to suffer.'*
> *As the place of execution may be accepted with great probability the*
> *Neronian Gardens on the Vatican, since there, according to Tacitus,*
> *were enacted in general the gruesome scenes of the Neronian*
> *persecution; and in this district, in the vicinity of the Via Cornelia*
> *and at the foot of the Vatican Hills, the Prince of the Apostles found*
> *his burial place.'*

This was the basis from which tradition grew, Simon Peter later being canonised as St Peter, the first Pope, with his reign listed as being between 32-67 CE.[13]

We are taught that the missionary journeys both Peter and Paul undertook, and the teachings they spread, laid the foundations of what today we know as the Europe-wide monotheistic religion of Christianity. Despite the persecutions, over the next 200 years Christianity spread progressively across the Roman Empire, an empire that contained within it a pantheon of gods and religious beliefs. Probably, because of the rebellion against Roman rule that had taken place in Palestine between 60 and 70 CE, Christians were not trusted by successive Emperors, and at various times Christians were subjected to further persecution on one pretext or another. Two hundred and fifty years after Nero – during the reign of the Roman Emperor, Diocletian – a new period of such ruthless persecutions began.

By 300 CE, the Roman Empire had become so vast and difficult to manage effectively that it was split into two administrative empires, one of the East and the other of the West. Diocletian was Emperor of the East.

There had been a number of setbacks in the empire, including an outbreak of plague. The death toll was so great that it significantly reduced the population in this part of the overall empire. The production of food had been affected, as had almost every other aspect of life, including the administration of the empire. Amongst the Roman hierarchy it was believed that the outbreak of plague had been caused by the intervention of the gods. Just as Nero had blamed the Christians for the great fire that engulfed Rome, so the Roman hierarchy under Diocletian blamed the Christians for this reversal of fortunes. Diocletian demanded that the Christians offer sacrifices to the Roman gods, under torture if necessary, in order to appease them. Diocletian's persecutions commenced in February 303 CE with the issue of an edict that resulted in Christian churches and places of worship being destroyed, and documents and manuscripts burnt, whilst bishops and leaders of Christian sects were tortured and imprisoned. It was a process that continued for a total of eight years. Until, that is, Constantine became Emperor.

There are many works associated with religion and history in which the claim is made that Constantine was born in England. According to modern historians, Constantine was born in February 272 CE (although some doubt remains about the accuracy of that date) in what today we know as the Balkan state of Serbia.[14] His full name was apparently Flavius Valerius Aurelius Constantinus. He is more usually referred to as Constantine I or Constantine the Great. His mother was named Helena, and his father was Constantius Chlorus, a highly regarded Roman general and an Emperor of the Roman Western Empire.

Constantine was well educated. He travelled to places such as Babylon (Iraq), Egypt and Palestine. He took an active role in political affairs of the empire and participated in wars in Persia, and in the Roman Empire border areas along the Danube. He was serving in Diocletian's court in 303 CE when Diocletian issued his first edict against the Christians. It is generally believed that Constantine fully participated in the persecution and suppression that then followed. It is difficult to imagine that an active politician and military officer in Diocletian's court at the time the edict was issued would not have fully participated in its execution, although he later denied such involvement.

Around 300 CE, Constantine's father, Chlorus, was given command of Iberia (Spain), Gaul (France) and Britain, one of the most northerly outposts of the Roman Empire. During this time Chlorus participated in several significant battles that resulted in victories in favour of Roman authority. Under Chlorus's rule, Christians were not persecuted in anything like the same ruthless manner that Diocletian was pursuing in the Eastern Empire. Constantine is recorded as having joined his father in Gaul and together they crossed into Britain and travelled to York, then a major Roman garrison town. Because of the cool, damp climate and conditions in Britain, a posting to these islands was, it seems, a Roman soldier's worst nightmare – a posting away from the warmth of southern Europe, the sophistication of Roman life, and the relative abundance of good food and wine. Chlorus became ill during his time in Britain and died at York in 306 CE, after which, the army apparently elected Constantine as Caesar, a position that would lead to his becoming Emperor.

Although historians note that Helena, Constantine's mother, was most probably born in the eastern Mediterranean, possibly in either modern Turkey or Bulgaria, there are also legends that connect her with Britain. It is this erroneous connection that probably led to the suggestion in earlier times that her son, Constantine, was born in England. Around 1100 CE, Geoffrey of Monmouth, a bishop of the Church of Wales, produced a work with the title *Historia Regum Britanniae – History of the Kings of Britain.* In this work he describes Helena as having been the daughter of a British king, Cole of Colchester.[15] Historians attribute much of Geoffrey of Monmouth's background material to earlier manuscripts produced by such writers as the Venerable Bede whose work *Historia Ecclesiastica Gentis Anglorum* had been written 400 years earlier, around 250 years after the withdrawal of the Romans from Britain. It is believed that Geoffrey of Monmouth confused Helena, mother of Constantine, with Elen, a lady associated with having founded Christian churches in Wales. She is also said to have been the wife of Magnus Maximus, a Roman general, who for a time was stationed in Britain, was declared Emperor, and died in 388 CE. It is believed that she also had a son whom she named Constantine. Elen later became known as St Helen of Caernarfon, a town in the north-west of Wales. It was the combined coincidences of her name, marriage to a Roman general who in turn became an emperor, and having a son whom she named Constantine that seems to have been the basis of the confusion created by Geoffrey of Monmouth and has led to the legends surrounding Helena's association with Britain. Notwithstanding that, Helena remains the patron saint of two towns in Britain: Abingdon in Oxfordshire and Colchester in Essex. Helena played a key role in the later establishment of Christianity within the Roman Empire.

By the time Constantine and his father had arrived in Britain in 305 CE, the fledgling new faith of Christianity had already been well established in the country. Tradition has it that Christianity first arrived around 40 CE, when the Church of Jerusalem, of which James the Lesser or James the Just was the first bishop, and from which Peter and Paul both set out on their respective missionary journeys, was still in its infancy and the Church of Rome was still many years from its first foundations. Joseph of Arimathea, a possible relative of the crucified Yehoshua, is believed to have landed on British shores at a place called Llantwit Major in South Wales.[16] This would coincide with the concept of the dispersal of key figures of the Church of Jerusalem on various missionary journeys such as those undertaken by Peter and Paul. A further belief exists that Christianity arrived through the influence of traders that sailed from the Mediterranean to Britain, or those fleeing Roman persecution after the Jewish uprising in Jerusalem between 66 and 70 CE. There is also some suggestion that the persecutions by Nero and Diocletian resulted in many Christians from Rome and the Eastern Empire relocating to Britain as a relative safe haven.

Thus by the time Constantine arrived with his father, Christianity had already been in Britain for some 250 years. It would be a further 250 years before the arrival of Austin the monk, later to be known as St Augustine of Canterbury, who is frequently, though misguidedly, credited with this missionary accolade. Tradition again has it that through the period that Constantine was in Britain, he became increasingly impressed by the peaceable nature, conviction and support for each other that Christians exhibited.

Following his departure from Britain as Augustus Caesar, Constantine faced severe challenges to his authority. The Roman Empires of the East and West were in some disarray. There were conflicts and quarrels between various contenders for the throne of Rome. Constantine was fully occupied defending the borders of Roman authority in northern Europe and took no part in the feuding that was taking place at the heart of the empire. Yet he was an Augustus and when he received news that statues erected in his honour were being overturned and destroyed, and that he was being branded as a tyrant, he had little option but to protect his reputation and position, and marched into Italy with his army of some 20,000 men. Needless to say, there were those seeking the throne of Rome that had access to far larger armies, often four or five times as many men as Constantine had at his disposal. As a result, his army was involved in several major battles, including at Susa, Turin and Verona, all of which resulted in victories for Constantine against overwhelming odds.

As Constantine continued his journey towards Rome, he apparently had a dream in which he saw that his salvation would come from marching under a banner carrying the symbol of the God of the Christians. At that time, the symbol was not the four armed cross of latter years; instead Constantine adopted the labarum, or chi-rho.

The Labarum

Although most of his army was comprised of believers in the pantheon of other gods celebrated within the Roman Empire, Constantine encouraged this symbol to be placed on the shields of his soldiers at the battle of Milvian Bridge, a bridge over the River Tiber, in October 312 CE. Constantine's opponent, Maxentius, died when he fell into the Tiber and drowned. Constantine attributed his success to support from the God of the Christians. Shortly after in 313 CE, he issued what has become known as the Edict of Milan, which to all intents and purposes was a proclamation of tolerance towards Christians and brought to an end the long years of brutal persecution. Although he continued to face challenges that were met on the battlefield, over the next decade Constantine increased his support in the empire, such that in 325 CE he became the indisputable holder of the throne of Rome and leader of the entire Roman Empire.

Meanwhile, a religious dispute had developed over many years between a deacon named Arius, and Peter, the Bishop of Alexandria. In simple terms, Arius disputed the divinity claimed by Jesus Christ as the Son of God, in a doctrine known as Arianism. There was much heated debate within the Church during which, at one stage, Arius was excommunicated and sent into exile, only to be reinstated later. It was not merely a local schism but extended amongst bishops right across the Roman Empire and beyond.

Constantine resolved to bring an end to the dispute and find a basis for religious peace that could unify the empire. He, in concert with Pope Sylvester, invited bishops from across the empire to assemble in Nicaea, encouraging them to do so by making state facilities available to them for transport and accommodation. According to the Catholic Encyclopedia, there were well over 250 bishops that ultimately attended. This meeting became known as the First Council of Nicaea. Discussions commenced in May 325 CE and became a more serious gathering in the following month of June, which also saw the arrival of the Emperor, Constantine. The Council continued until August 325 CE. There was great debate about the dispute started by Arius. In the end Arianism was denounced. Arius's writings, books and concepts were cast into fires. The key result for the religion of Christianity was the issue of a declaration that has passed through the subsequent ages as the Nicene Creed. Thus the Roman Catholic religion was created and adopted for the Roman Empire, its doctrine having been formalised at the First Council of Nicaea in 325 CE. Gradually over the next few centuries, churches and monasteries were founded across Europe, and in all the countries surrounding or bordering the Mediterranean. Arianism, however, did not disappear and remained an undercurrent of belief in the territories that were not totally subservient to Roman domination.

Having seized the throne of Rome and been instrumental in encouraging the Council of Nicaea, both in 325 CE, Constantine went on to develop Byzantium as the centre of the Roman Empire, based in a city he called New Rome, a city whose name was changed to Constantinople after his death. In 330 CE, he transferred the official administrative responsibilities to New Rome, and in so doing, founded what 18th century academics called the Byzantine Empire, although in reality it was still the Roman Empire. It was an empire that was to hold sway over much of Eastern Europe, North Africa and the Middle East for the next 1000 years, with Constantinople developing as a centre of trade, strategically placed between the Mediterranean and Black Seas, and a link between Europe and Asia. Constantinople fell to the forces of the Ottoman Empire in 1453.

Around 450 CE, the armies of the Western Roman Empire were defeated and the city of Rome collapsed. The defensive Roman Legions that had occupied much of Europe, North Africa and Asia Minor withdrew, along with most of the regional administrators. In Europe, this vacuum was replaced over the next few centuries by a series of small tribal kingdoms.

Thus, when the military-based Roman Empire and administration was finally destroyed around 450 CE, the ground was prepared for a new form of government, based on religious doctrine, theologically directed as the Roman Church with its headquarters still based in Rome.

As noted above, it was shortly before the fall of Rome that the Emperor Constantine formalised Christianity as the primary religion of the empire. At a time when the Roman Empire was in danger of fragmenting, just as during his time in England, Constantine became impressed by the attitude of those citizens who were believers in what was then a new faith system. He sought to harness it as a way of binding the people of the empire together.

The dogma, organisational structure and content of the New Testament of the Bible as we have come to know it were formalised at the First Council of Nicaea in 325 CE. Most of that dogma and structure remain in place at the start of the 21st century, nearly 2000 years after it was prescribed. It was from this Council that the basis of the Roman Church that was to dominate much of Europe through the Middle Ages was founded.

Over the few hundred years following the Council of Nicaea, Roman Christianity extended its reach across Europe, replacing the gods and belief systems that our ancestors had developed over hundreds, maybe even thousands, of generations. These earlier belief systems were based substantially on the natural world that surrounded them, a world which provided people with all the means for survival. In particular, there was universal worship and respect for the sun and the moon. This was found even in the Roman Empire. The cult of Sol Invictus was a worship of the Sun God, practised by no lesser a person than Constantine himself. These non-Christian belief systems became known as paganism and over the next few centuries they were ruthlessly demonised by the expanding Roman Church.

As the Roman Church extended its influence across Europe so a controlling and administrative structure needed to be put in place. Even prior to the Council of Nicaea, the basic structure had been devised with bishops, deacons and priests. The role of the bishop became much more than merely spreading the concept and doctrine of Christianity. It became a powerful role in maintaining law and order, and mediating in disputes. We get some idea of their power and influence on society at that time in the following extract from the Catholic Encyclopedia:

'...the Roman Empire, now Christian, granted bishops other powers. They were exclusively empowered to take cognizance of the misdemeanours of clerics, and every lawsuit entered into against the latter had to be brought before the bishop's court. The Emperor Constantine often permitted all Christians to carry their lawsuits *before the bishop, but this right was withdrawn at the end of the fourth century. Nevertheless, they continued to act as arbitrators, which office the earliest Christians had committed to them. More important, perhaps, is the part which the Roman law assigns to the bishops as protectors of the weak and oppressed. The master was permitted to legally emancipate his slave in the bishop's presence; the latter had also the power to remove young girls from immoral houses where their parents or masters had placed them, and to restore them to liberty. Newly born infants abandoned by their parents were legally adjudged to those who sheltered them, but to avoid abuses it was required that the bishop should certify that the child was a foundling. The Roman law allowed the bishops the right to visit prisons at their discretion for the purpose of improving the condition of prisoners and of ascertaining whether the rules in favour of the latter were observed. The bishops possessed great influence over the Christian emperors...'[17]*

The bishops even had the power to exercise authority over literature and thereby what people were taught. The power and respect for the bishops continued to grow long after the collapse of Rome. They held ranks in society akin to princes, dukes and lords. Indeed some even assumed such titles. As time passed and their influence grew so they acquired thrones – the bishop's throne – which in Britain and France were housed in great cathedrals. And many of them became extremely wealthy.

Charlemagne and the Rise of the Holy Roman Empire

Well before the final collapse of Rome as the dominant centre of the Roman Empire, its armies were constantly harassed by groups of tribes, especially in the north and north-east, who refused to succumb to Roman domination. Principal among these tribes were the Goths, later defined in history as the Barbarians. They were not a people without a culture or influence of their own. Neither did they lack leadership. They defeated Roman armies in a number of significant battles and even captured the capital, Byzantium. Their religious beliefs were originally pagan, but as Christianity spread so they converted to Arianism, the religious doctrine of Arius that was cast aside at the Council of Nicaea during the formalisation of the Roman Church. The influence of the Goths spread until they became identifiable as two separate entities: the Goths to the north, and the Visigoths who inhabited the area that we know today as the Iberian peninsula and south-west France. It was the Visigoths who ultimately brought about the defeat and collapse of the city of Rome.

During this period, groups or tribes of Germanic peoples from an area to the east of the River Rhine moved further west and settled in areas that today we know as Belgium and the Netherlands. These peoples have become known in history as the Franks. The Roman Empire, at that time, still had considerable military influence across Europe and a hundred years prior to Constantine securing the throne of Rome, Roman armies were attempting to remove the newcomers. Finally, in 359 CE, Constantine's nephew, Julian, fought a significant battle against them, which was marked by a major Roman victory. After that, we are told, the Franks settled peacefully and even supplied mercenaries to fight in the Roman army.

One of the last great battles fought by the Romans against the Barbarians included an army of Franks led by a man named Merovech. From him, and his name, came a line of Frankish kings and dynasties known to history as the Merovingians. Merovech had a son, known to us as Childeric, who in turn went on to have a son, Clovis. Tradition has it that Clovis was a holder of pagan beliefs, but also became a Roman Christian, thereby allying himself more closely with the Roman Empire based at Constantinople in Byzantium for political purposes. Clovis then went on to cultivate the support and leadership of the Franks and secure the territories they occupied. In so doing he laid the foundations for the Merovingian kingdom. It was not a small kingdom. As one authoritative writer notes:

> 'Clovis's kingdom was immense in extent, a testimony to the extraordinary energy and administrative genius of the man. In

modern terms, he had conquered all of France, all of the Low Countries, all of Switzerland, most of Germany as far as the Elbe (with the exception of a Saxon enclave around modern Hanover which would give Charlemagne a lifetime's problem). He had added Burgundy and Bavaria and most of Aquitaine – all quite distinct entities – to what was now known as Frankia or Frankland, the name 'Gaul' already receding into history. He had no one capital but moved his court, as need required, from Metz to Orleans, from Paris to Cologne or Soissons.'[18]

Clovis, who had acquired the Merovingian throne in 481 CE, built a kingdom that was to be a dominant force in Western Europe until the end of the 7th century. In the latter years it witnessed some of the excesses that can also be observed in the Roman Empire, whereby emperors, determined to secure the throne of Rome, eliminated any potential usurpers by assassination, even to the extent of murdering entire families as well. So it was that the Merovingians were undermined by sections of the wider family murdering other family members in a bid for the throne of the Franks, until the family power and influence rested with fewer and fewer individuals who were ultimately defeated by other more powerful families. Thus came the turn of the Carolingians to rule over the Franks and to hold sway and influence over European events. Amongst their number was Pepin the Short, and later his son, Prince Charles, more widely known as the Emperor Charlemagne. The court of the Carolingians was based in Aachen, today a city just inside Germany, over the border with Belgium.

For one to be deemed a knight, a ceremony of official recognition needed to be performed. This has traditionally been seen as being dubbed by a sword, with the ceremony being undertaken by a ruling monarch; that is, the monarch placing the flat blade of a sword on the shoulders of the person being conferred with the title 'knight'. Until the arrival of the Carolingians the title 'king' was more a definition of tribal leadership. Several historical writers note that in Europe, following the formalisation of Christianity, a king was a person who effectively reported directly to the Pope. That person was elected within a tribe and would be ceremonially *raised* to their office. This was done by possibly 12 strong warriors who formed into a tight circle. They set their shields horizontally to form a platform. The young warriors would then lift the platform of shields just above the ground, with their left arms, such that the man who was to become their king stood above them. The highly acclaimed historical writer, Russell Chamberlin, notes:

> *'The chief would stand upon its wobbling surface as the young men raised him high. It was a simple and obvious ceremony of profound and subtle significance. It showed that the tribe realised that there must be one man above the rest and he had to be raised up so that all could see him. But he was supported by the strong left arms of his fellows... He was not their ruler, but the first among equals; if they withdrew the support of their arms he would fall to the ground.'*[19]

It was, continues Chamberlin, a perfect symbol of their commitment to their leader, and him to them. What is immediately obvious in this process is that it was a democratic decision. The leader, the king, was raised to his office by the consent of his tribe. It was not necessarily a hereditary line of succession as so many kingdoms later became. The *raising* tradition gave way to a more formal process of *anointment* – a process that involved being marked in some way by an application of holy oil. Christianity was derived from the traditions of the Hebrews. In the Old Testament there is a passage where Samuel meets the young man, David, later to become King David, father of Solomon. It reads:

> *'Then Samuel took the horn of oil, and anointed him in the midst of his brothers...'*   Samuel 16:13

Thus was the same process used by the Roman Church for the anointment of subsequent monarchs.

It was logical that if the King was to report to the Pope, then the anointing process needed to be undertaken by an approved emissary of the Pope – the Bishop. It is believed that Pepin was one of the first kings in Europe to achieve his status in this way, around 740 CE, at Soissons in northern France. His status was greatly enhanced a few years later.

As mentioned earlier, the Roman Emperor Constantine had relocated the centre of Roman administration to Constantinople in 330 CE. Although the Roman Empire that had for centuries dominated much of Europe, North Africa, the Middle East and Asia Minor collapsed after the invasion of Rome by the Barbarians (Visigoths), a Roman-Byzantine Empire still existed and held considerable sway over the area we know as Italy, whilst Rome, the place of execution of the early Christian missionaries Peter and Paul, remained the centre for Roman Christian religious administration.

In the 6th century, the Lombards, tribes that had lived along the Danube valleys, were moulded into a strong administrative and military force in much the same way that the Franks had been moulded into a nation of peoples by Merovech, Childeric and Clovis. Over the next 200 years the Lombards conquered most of Italy. Even as early as the 750s CE, the Lombards had seized territories surrounding Rome that had belonged to the Roman Church. The ownership of the land, and the revenues they generated for the Church, had originated through the 'Law of Constantine' in which the Emperor Constantine the Great granted the Roman Church the right to hold possessions of land. Wealthy Roman families, seeking to improve their prospects of a divine afterlife, donated lands such that by the mid-8th century the holdings the Church had at its disposal were quite substantial, embracing entire towns with castles and fortifications, and yielding a considerable income to the Pope's treasury. In their march through Italy, the Lombards had seized several such holdings and threatened Rome itself. The Pope and his senior officials fled across the Alps in 754 CE, seeking refuge in the Frankish kingdom ruled by the Carolingian Pepin – Pepin the Short, father of Charles, the later Emperor Charlemagne. The Pope was also motivated to seek military support against the Lombards, to recapture the lost properties and, no doubt, the revenues they provided.

In return for their support, Pope Stephen II offered several inducements to Pepin. Amongst these were:

- being crowned by Pope Stephen II himself, including his two sons and his wife, in the great church of St Denis, now just to the north of Paris;
- being bestowed with the title Patrician of the Romans.

Both of these titles were hugely significant. Pepin's kingdom was by no means secure. He had had a brother, Carloman, and when their father, Charles Martel, had died, the Frankish kingdom had been divided between them which had led to all manner of complications. Carloman had died of natural causes and Pepin had inherited the entire kingdom again, but it was not yet settled. In addition, he had made other conquests outside of the traditional Frankish border. To add to the complications he was also connected to the Lombards by marriage. Being crowned by Pope Stephen made it clear that Pepin had the full support of the Roman Church, and sanctioned him as the rightful king. The title of Patrician was even more significant for, amongst other privileges, it bestowed on him the honour of being the head of Rome's wealthiest families and nobility. It was an honour that the Pope alone could not bestow, but required the approbation of the citizens of Rome, and they had given that approval in anticipation of Pepin's promise to protect them from the Lombards. It was yet another endorsement of his kingship and of his family. The combined significance would not be lost on the Lombards. For the Pope and the Roman Church it had the benefit of securing the services of a strong military force to help ensure its protection.

Thus, crowned and honoured, in 755 CE Pepin led an army, together with the Pope and his entourage, into Italy. By success on the battlefield and negotiation he was able to secure all the properties of the Roman Church which were then in Lombard hands, and an undertaking that there would be no further attacks on Rome. Having secured such agreements, Pepin returned to his kingdom. The Lombards, however, failed to honour their obligations. The Pope again sent for Pepin who, history tells, had only just returned home. Thus, in 756 CE, Pepin marched his army over the Alps again. This time he drove the Lombards out, extending still further the size of the Frankish Empire. Pepin sent messengers to secure the keys to the various cities that formed part of the properties held by the Church, and took them, along with magistrates and other hierarchy, to Rome where he drew up new deeds for the cities, and then, the Catholic Encyclopedia tells us, he had them placed on the tomb of St Peter.[20] Through these actions, Pepin established what have become known as the States of the Church.

The role of the Franks in the service to the Pope did not go down well with the Roman-Byzantine Empire based in Constantinople. In wresting control of territories from the Lombards, Pepin had effectively taken over some of the last vestiges of the empire then remaining in Italy, leaving the former Roman Empire of the East with a few outposts on the Adriatic coast of eastern Italy, territories that could be easily serviced by the Byzantine navy. Amongst such outposts were places that would later take names that we know today, such as Venice.

The Roman Church had until that time continued to show allegiance to the Roman Emperor who was based in the residual Roman Empire of the East. The land and properties that Pepin secured for the church as the States of the Church were in effect the last residual lands of the former Roman Empire of the West that had been based in Rome. In theory, the Roman Church was still a function of the Roman Empire based in Constantinople; as such, the Pope, although the head of authority in the Roman Christian religion, was nevertheless a mere functionary of the empire and subservient to the Emperor. The problem with this situation was that the role and influence of the Roman Emperor over affairs in a Europe, dominated by the rule of the Franks, was extremely limited. Since 450 CE, there had been a consistent contraction of the Roman

Empire so that its territorial control was limited to a small area at the eastern end of the Mediterranean Sea. Militarily, the Roman Empire was no longer in a position to protect the Roman Christian church that it had founded, let alone the lands and properties that made up the States of the Church. The end result was that the Roman Christian church moved its allegiance from the east to the west. The Catholic Encyclopedia comments as follows:

> '...the papacy threw off the political ties that bound it to the East and entered into new relations with the West, which made possible the development of the new Western civilization.' [21]

Pepin the Short, King of the Franks, Patrician of the Romans and many other titles, died in 768 CE. The control of the kingdom of the Franks, together with his titles, transferred to his son, Prince Charles.

When Clovis had first moulded the various tribes of the Franks into a cohesive nation he did so as a Christian. All his successors – up to and including Pepin the Short – had followed the same religious path. The expansionist course followed by Pepin resulted in more and more subjects being converted from their pagan beliefs to the mainstream beliefs that formed Roman Christianity. Charles pursued a similar course, though a little more rigorously.

Charles was almost constantly at war for some 45 years of his reign. During that time he not only had to contend with rebellious factions within the kingdom, but with wars and skirmishes along his kingdom's borders with other tribal groupings, especially in the north and east. Chief amongst these were the pagan Saxons, who held territory to the east of the River Rhine. For years, there seemed to be an endless round of wars with the Saxons. Each time he defeated them he would offer an ultimatum – death, or they could be baptised as Christians. Needless to say, most opted for baptism. No sooner did he leave them than they were back to their pagan ways. Eventually, in order to suppress them and to ensure they followed the Christian religion, Charlemagne ordered one of the greatest forced migrations of history. He compelled large numbers of Saxons to move into, and be distributed around, the original Frankish kingdom, whilst he moved Franks into territories that had formerly been held by the Saxons. By the time of his death, Charlemagne's kingdom of the Franks extended from the borders of Denmark in the north to northern Spain in the south, and from the Atlantic Ocean and North Sea coasts in the west to the rivers Elbe and Danube in the east, including most of northern Italy. It was a massive territory that constituted the bulk of Western Europe – and the prevailing religion throughout was Roman Christianity.

Just as his father had received the title of Patrician of the Romans in return for service that he provided to Pope Stephen II, so Charles would receive another title from a grateful Pope, a title that cemented Western Europe and the kingdom of the Franks to the Roman Church.

In 799 CE, Pope Leo was forced to flee across the Alps to seek help from the King of the Franks and Patrician of the Romans, who at that time was based at Paderborn, a town not far from Aachen. He explained to Charles that he had been brutally attacked and an attempt had been made to gouge out his eyes and tear out his tongue. This had happened whilst he was in a church procession in Rome – the attack having been undertaken by a group of ruffians in the pay of his two nephews, who themselves were accompanying Leo. Knowing the Pope was with the King of the Franks, the two nephews wrote to Charles and acknowledged their part in the attack, stating that it had been undertaken because the Pope had debased his office through a number of alleged crimes.

In theory, it was an issue to be dealt with by the Roman Emperor based in Constantinople, but, as mentioned earlier, the Roman-Byzantine Empire had severely contracted and was in no real position to offer the judicial support that Leo needed.

Accompanied by several of Charles's aides, Leo returned to Rome where he faced trial for the crimes alleged by his nephews. The Pope was found innocent, which meant that his two nephews, by owning up to their actions in their correspondence with Charles, were found guilty. Sentence of the two nephews was delayed until Charles, as Patrician of the Romans, arrived in Rome in December 800 CE. The nephews were sentenced to death for treason, but following a request by Leo, this was commuted to life imprisonment.

As it was December, Charles took advantage of being in Rome to attend a mass in St Peter's on Christmas Day. He apparently attended in the traditional dress associated with his office as Patrician of the Romans. Whilst Charles was kneeling and saying prayers, the Pope, in what seems to have been a well-rehearsed manoeuvre, and without any previous hint to Charles about what was to come, approached him and placed on his head the imperial crown of Rome. The last such official wearer had been Romulus Augustus, 325 years earlier, at the final collapse of Rome in 476 CE. In that one act on 25 December 800 CE, Charlemagne was effectively crowned as Emperor and King of the Romans.

Needless to note, this did not go down well with the Roman-Byzantine Empire in Constantinople. In their eyes, there was already an emperor. They alone, they believed, had the legal right to appoint and anoint their emperors. Historians note that, legally, they were right. The problem was that there was considerable turmoil in Constantinople. First, they had tried to encourage a relationship with disaffected Lombards to militarily reclaim territories in Italy that the Byzantine Empire had lost. They were soundly defeated by the Franks, and it became clear to the Roman-Byzantine rulers that the opportunity to regain such territories in the future seemed extremely remote. Thus their influence over the affairs of the Roman Church was practically non-existent. Secondly, there was a great deal of infighting for the position of emperor, reminiscent of the murder and mayhem that had preceded the earlier collapse of the Imperial Roman Empire, based in Rome.

Constantine V had married a Greek by the name of Irene and had a son. Constantine V died when his son was still very young. The title of emperor passed to the son but being too young to rule in his own right, Irene became Regent, and as such, co-emperor. By the time he was a young man in his early twenties, the young

Constantine was seeking his own power base and to take a more direct control over affairs of state. His mother clearly liked the power she had wielded for so long and thus a power struggle broke out between them. It ended with Irene being the victor, gruesomely maiming her own son so that he could never resist her again, followed in 799 CE, by her being proclaimed Augusta Irene. In the eyes of the Franks and the Roman Church hierarchy, a woman as Augusta dictated that there was no emperor.

The crowning and anointing of Charles as Emperor solidified the relationship of the Roman Church to developments in Western Europe. Charlemagne, Charles King of the Franks, died in 814 CE. The vast kingdom he and his father, Pepin, had created passed to his three sons. They were unable to retain the influence of their forebears, and a few years later it all began to unravel.

For many earlier historians, the territories of the Frankish kingdom controlled by Charlemagne when he became Emperor were defined as the Holy Roman Empire. Later historians decreed that it was not holy for it was not directly ruled over by the Pope; that it was not Roman because it was the extended kingdom of the Franks; and that it was not an Empire. The shape of the empire changed over the centuries that followed, many of the successive emperors being crowned in Aachen, the main centre of Carolingian Frankish rule. The Holy Roman Empire officially ceased to exist following the French Revolution at the end of the 18th century and the rise to power of Napoleon Bonaparte. He apparently declared that he was not a successor to the deposed French king, Louis, but of Charlemagne. In so doing he was attempting to claim rule over the Holy Roman Empire. The historian Russell Chamberlin writes:

> 'Two years later, on 6 August 1806, Francis II, the true emperor, abdicated under pressure, releasing all states from their oath of allegiance. So ended the empire, 1006 years after Charlemagne received its crown.' [22]

Charlemagne's Influence on the Military Development of Knights

It was during the Carolingian period, and Charlemagne's reign in particular, that a number of the separate elements attributed to knighthood previously mentioned came together to enable the military superiority that the Carolingians demonstrated over their enemies. To have come together, in so far that their time was right, is one thing. To have the intuition and imagination to use them is something else, for it means deserting methods with which one has become familiar, methods that are therefore known, tried and tested.

For centuries both before and after Charlemagne it was the foot soldier that bore the brunt of battle. Horses, and horses and chariots, although used, were few by comparison with the sheer numbers of men that could be assembled for relatively little cost as foot soldiers. Horses and chariots were ideal for fast skirmishes, but it was the ranks of the foot soldiers that had to meet their opponents in hand-to-hand combat. The man on a horse, or the archer in a chariot, could launch a single missile such as a javelin or arrow, and gallop away hardly aware as to who his victim may have been. The foot soldier, however, would come face to face with his opponent, see the fear in his eyes, feel the sword grind against bone as it tore into flesh, the warmth of spilled blood over his hands and the last gasping breaths as he terminated a life, and then move on to another potential victim. That, historians tell us, is how it was at the start of the Carolingian period.

Just as the Romans and Greeks before them had done, the Carolingians established schools. The type of education received was not that associated with reading, writing, literature, numeracy and the subjects that later became classified as the liberal arts; those subjects were taught at cathedral or monastic schools. No, the schools noted here were military training centres where the strategies of war were taught, techniques of battle were honed, weapon skills practised, and, from time to time, new ideas and concepts tested and rehearsed.

As Pepin and Charlemagne extended their kingdoms they occasionally came into contact with different strategies and weapons, some of which they could modify to their own advantage. The Lombards, for example, who so often provided difficulties for Pepin, were apparently excellent horsemen. They bred horses and used them effectively. Most of the mounted warriors rode bare-back and hence were relatively easy to dislodge and disable. Charlemagne recognised the value of cavalry and cultivated it as part of his strategic resources.

It was around this time that a new development enhanced the capability of the mounted warrior. The stirrup arrived in Europe and Charlemagne was quick to see its benefits. The simple device and structure of the stirrup provided several advantages, one of which was the ability of the warrior to stand up above one's opponents, hacking down on them with a sword, on both sides of the animal, a feat not easy otherwise. A second advantage was in the use of an extended javelin known as the lance. With a javelin one was not sure if, once thrown, it had had any effect. One either needed to carry a supply of javelins, or run the risk of having to dismount and retrieve any that could be found – a highly risky business. Furthermore, carrying more than two javelins at any one time posed its own problems, so, once spent, time had to be taken out of the fight by returning to a holding point and collecting more. The lance, on the other hand, was more effective. Longer than the javelin, it could be directed at a single individual, perhaps a chief or leader. Holding and guiding the lance whilst it did its job meant it was targeted. On a horse ridden bare-back, this produced other problems. With a horse at full gallop and the lance hitting a relatively static individual, the lance would go right through its target. The sheer force of impact would result in the rider being thrown off the back of the horse and very probably sustaining death or injury himself. Alternatively, strategic timing meant letting go of the lance at the moment of impact with a need to return, dismount and try to pull it from the remains of the victim, again leaving the horseman highly vulnerable. So the Carolingians modified their lances by adding a straight piece of metal just beneath the point of the lance. Thus, when the tip of the lance impacted the victim, it did not go right through the body but to just a sufficient depth to enable their immobilisation. Standing in the stirrups also meant that the lance could be directed at the victim at a more acute angle and, by firmly grasping the shaft, the passing speed of the horse would result more often than not in the lance being withdrawn from the victim and therefore being almost immediately available for use again.

Through the combined effect of the Carolingians' use of massed cavalry, the stirrup and the modified lance, battlefield efficiency was considerably advanced in their favour. One thing, however, had not changed. Horses were expensive to keep, rear and equip, which meant that the cavalry would have remained the domain of the aristocrat.

As well as the cavalry, Charlemagne placed great store on armour. He expressly forbid the export of the mailed shirt or any other form of mailed or armoured protection. It was an edict that he continuously reminded his people of. Anyone caught trying to export such armour would have had their property confiscated. This may seem relatively lenient today, but it could mean death for an entire family. With everything one owns being removed, the opportunities to work, to feed one's family, to have currency, are gone. It was a draconian measure and people in those times would have realised the significance of it. Thus, his warriors, and especially the aristocrats who served in the cavalry, retained modest protection.

The Germanic Emperor
Historians note that at the end of Charlemagne's rein there were effectively two major groups of peoples – the Franks in the west, substantially descended from the original peoples that had moved to the area of north-west Europe long before Constantine the Great gained the throne of Rome, and those who were descended from the Saxons and Germanic tribes who came from the area east of the Rhine and had been absorbed through the expansion of the Frankish kingdom over a period of some 400 years, from the time of Clovis to Charlemagne. Ruling the vast kingdom proved difficult for Charlemagne and he installed some of his sons as kings to rule over parts of the overall kingdom. His son, Pepin, was installed as King

of Italy, and Louis I as King of Aquitaine. Pepin, the elder of the two brothers, died a few years prior to Charlemagne, so the title of Emperor passed to Louis.

Although a large territory may share a common language, local dialects can exist within the language, influenced in some cases by isolation, conquest or contact through trade. Fifty years after the crowning of Charlemagne as Emperor, we find that not only were there the kingdoms of Italy and Aquitaine, but new kingdoms had been created, including those of the King of the East Franks (East Francia) and King of the West Franks (West Francia), whilst the title 'Emperor' had been passed to Charlemagne's grandson, Lothar I. With this diversity of kingdoms we also find differentiating clusters of language. And with differing kingdoms there came conflict and disagreement. The first great Union of Europe, created by Charlemagne, became divided.

One hundred years after the death of Charlemagne his great-great-great grandson became Henry I in what had been the Kingdom of East Francia. History records him as the first king of the Germans, having done much to unite the separate Germanic tribes and dukedoms that had existed within the Carolingian kingdom. He also inherited the title 'Emperor'. According to historians, at his coronation he refused to be anointed, wishing his reign to be on the basis of the acclamation of the people, not by subservience to the Roman Church.

On his death, his son became king, Otto I, the Great. He continued and strengthened the German kingdom. As a great-great-great-great grandson of Charlemagne, he had insisted that his coronation be undertaken at Aachen, the city his famous ancestor had used as the capital of his kingdom. Just as had been the case in the time of Pepin and Charlemagne, the Pope of the Church of Rome, Pope John XII, was experiencing difficulties with factional fighting and territorial incursions. He sought assistance from Otto, offering him the Imperial Crown of Rome in return. Otto crossed the Alps as his two famous forebears had done. On 2 February 962 CE, Otto was crowned King of the Romans. As Emperor, he was seen as being invested with the title Emperor of the Western Roman Empire, a title that had been unclaimed since the death of Julius Nepos in 480 CE. Otto is therefore considered by some as the first Holy Roman Emperor. Nevertheless, lists of Holy Roman Emperors start with Charlemagne in 800-814 CE. Otto I (936-973 CE) is eleventh on the list.

We have seen that Clovis and the Merovingians created a kingdom that became known as Frankia or Frankland from which the name of the country we know as France has been derived. We have also seen that the Carolingians, Pepin and Charlemagne in particular, did much to suppress paganism and spread the acceptance of Christianity, as espoused through the Roman Church, across Western Europe. The symbol of veneration in the Roman Church is the Virgin Mary. By going to the aid of popes, and thereby the Church, when called on to do so, by reclaiming properties from the Lombards, by instigating the structure of the States of the Church, Pepin and Charlemagne were in effect assisting a 'damsel in distress'.

A further image so often associated with knights is that of St George slaying a dragon. Many historians consider this image to be an allegorical representation of knights defending the Roman Church against its enemies. It therefore has overtones of a connection between Pepin and Charlemagne on the one hand, and the later era of the Crusades on the other.

But what of the title 'knight'?

The Romances

Charlemagne was a hugely charismatic character, as was Otto I over a hundred years later. Various writers consider Charlemagne to be the originator of Orders of Knights through the use of the word 'paladin'.

As Charlemagne and his predecessors gained new territories, it was appropriate to reward those of his court that had served him well with areas of land, and, in some cases, titles to go with them. Such landowners were required to supply at least one man, fully equipped with a horse, armour, sword and lance, to fight with

Charlemagne's army. Most of these recruits were the sons of the landowner, so in the traditions of the Roman Equestrian Order they were from the wealthiest and most noble families of the Carolingian kingdom. It was normal in those times that a small group of trusted individuals would become a bodyguard, protecting their leader. This was usually a close-knit group of 12 men who would be invested by the king for that purpose. It is to these mounted warriors that the title 'paladin' may be directed, referring to a champion or warrior, the same connotation given to a knight.

It is also worth remembering that the term 'knight' is an English word, whereas the function is derived from the French equivalent of *chevalier*, which in turn is associated with the French *cheval* – the word for 'horse'.

From the 9th century onwards, a string of poems evolved, all extolling the adventures of various warriors from the Carolingian period. Having developed in French and German and later being taken up in England, they are the stories that contributed to the popular image of King Arthur and the Knights of the Round Table; the exploits of Sir Galahad; the *Song of Roland*, and many more. These fictional poems and stories are referred to as the Romances, and it seems that it is the form of the Romances that has created the illusion and imagery surrounding 'knights of old'. Yet in the background of history there are a number of events that came together and have been moulded into that imagery.

We have seen how, through the involvement of Popes Leo and John, the Roman Church was bound up in the development of Western Europe in what later became known as the Holy Roman Empire. Through Charlemagne and his forebears we see the coming together of the basic elements that characterise the imagery of the knight – the fearless mounted warrior dressed in armour, with sword or lance at the ready. Legend promotes the image of one 'good knight' – the *chevalier* – above all others.

The Tales of King Arthur and the Knights of the Round Table
The concept of 'chivalry' suggests in the minds of many people an age of long, long ago, before that of the Knights of the Round Table. With larger-than-life characters like Sir Lancelot and Sir Galahad there is a suggestion that the concept of knighthood was already in existence before their adventures began. The question this raises is when was that and when was the era of the Knights of the Round Table?

In the tales of King Arthur, his fabled city and castle are called Camelot. Depending on the era of the mythology, the site of Camelot is associated with numerous different locations in Britain. Amongst these are Caerleon near Newport, South Wales, the former site of a Roman fortress; Tintagel Castle on the Cornish coast; Colchester in Essex; the cathedral city of Winchester, the ancient capital of Wessex and home to King Alfred; and Glastonbury in Somerset, to name but a few. Arthur is also said to have been, separately, both a king of the Welsh and the English. Some researchers suggest that he may have been buried in what is today a small wood near Wall, a town near Birmingham, a site suggested as a possible burial site of early English kings.[23] Other popular mythology has King Arthur having been buried in Wales or at Glastonbury. This last piece of mythology seems to derive from the 14th century at a time when Glastonbury Abbey was experiencing considerable financial problems and the monks were looking for ways to improve their income. They declared that they had found the grave of King Arthur and clearly defined the spot within the grounds of the abbey, after which Glastonbury Abbey became a popular site of pilgrimage. Needless to note, the financial plight of the abbey was greatly relieved – it soon became considerably wealthy.

So where and how did this diverse perception of King Arthur and the Knights of the Round Table evolve?

It seems that around the time of the First Crusade in 1099 CE, several poets and troubadours wove fact about the exploits of the early knights into tales of fiction. In the Middle Ages literacy was not widespread across the populace of Europe, so historic events and characters of significance were wrapped up in stories that could be memorised and passed on in a verbal tradition. They were the stories of folklore. In continental Europe, such stories surrounded the Emperor Charlemagne and the exploits of the warriors that supported him. In Wales there was a series of such stories about the period following the Roman presence in Britain, of Welsh princes, princesses and various tribal leaders and the battles they fought. The troubadours of the 12th century may well have picked up elements of those early stories and then woven into them new adventures. These new poems and stories are now known as the Grail Romances – stories and folklore surrounding a quest for the holy grail and the exploits of heroes in the characters of knights.

King Arthur made his appearance in the 13th century in a work entitled *The History of the Kings of England* written by Geoffrey of Monmouth, although there is no historical evidence that any such person existed. Although it is cited as an historical work, academics place little credence on it, being uncertain whether Geoffrey was drawing on sources that he had available at that time and have since been lost, or if it was a work of fiction. It seems clear, however, that at the time it was completed, around 1135 CE, it became a very popular source and work of reference. So popular were the stories of Arthur that he also appears in some European tales that developed around the same time. Such was his fame that in the early 16th century a statue to King Arthur was erected near Innsbruck, Austria.[24]

The Round Table makes its first appearance in Robert Wace's *Roman de Brut*, possibly written in 1155 CE, 20 years after the work by Geoffrey. There is a famous Round Table that hangs in the Great Hall in Winchester Castle, on which is depicted an image of King Arthur, implying a connection between the table and Arthurian mythology. Yet that table is dated to the end of the 13th century, possibly about 1290 CE, nearly 150 years after Robert Wace's work.

A few years after Wace's introduction of the Round Table, around 1170 CE, we find the works of Chrétien de Troyes – stories that introduce us to the character of Lancelot. At the time these works were produced, Chrétien de Troyes was serving at the court of the

Count of Champagne, a descendant from Charlemagne and from a line of nobility closely associated with the Knights Templar and the Crusades. The stories about the Crusades and heroic deeds that must have abounded at the court, along with the coming and going of actual prominent knights of that era, must surely have been a rich source of inspiration for his stories.

Around 1225 CE, we find the Arthurian stories of Parzival appearing in Germany, written by Wolfram von Echenbach. Parzival translates to the knight Percival in English versions. Interconnected with these tales is the mythology promulgated by the monks at Glastonbury Abbey following their miraculous discovery of the supposed grave of Arthur.

Yet the real popularity of King Arthur, his favoured knights and the imagery of the Round Table owes perhaps more to the printing press, invented by William Caxton in 1485 CE. It was the combination of this invention, plus the stories of King Arthur written by Sir Thomas Malory, that turned folklore into literature, leaving us with the defined imagery that survives today. Malory lived in the 15th century and completed his famous work *Morte d'Arthur (Death of Arthur)* around 1465 CE. It is a work that brings together all the elements of the Arthurian legend as a single Grail Romance. A document known as the Winchester Manuscript was discovered in the library of Winchester College in the 1930s. Close examination by eminent academics suggests that this manuscript was actually in Caxton's printing works when the printed edition of Malory's works was being produced in 1485 CE. Malory apparently produced his original works as a series of short but interrelated stories. Caxton, it is believed, compiled them as a single volume, organised them into chapters and gave the finished work the title of *Morte d'Arthur.*

What we see from all this is that the popular imagery we have of Arthur and the Knights of the Round Table developed over a sustained period of time, culminating perhaps in the revolutionary invention of the printing press. The Arthurian legends were so strong that they even had an impact on certain events in later English history.

The Wars of the Roses were a series of conflicts fought over a period of 30 years from 1455 to 1485 CE between two branches of a family, known as the houses of York and Lancaster, both branches being descended from Edward III. The House of York used an emblem of a white rose, whilst the Lancastrians were represented by the red rose.

This conflict was really about the precedence of the line of descent to the throne of England being through either the male or female lines. The House of York claimed descent from the second surviving son of Edward III, but through the female line. Henry IV was the founder of the Lancastrian dynasty who claimed descent from John of Gaunt, the third son of Edward III, and through the male line.

Henry VI was a descendant of the House of Lancaster. He was not a strong king, lost most of the English territories held in France, and suffered from a medical complaint that led to a form of insanity or nervous breakdown. During this period, the House of York grew in power and influence which ultimately led to the king being arrested, imprisoned in the Tower of London and eventually murdered, at which stage the House of York was able to seize the throne.

The Wars of the Roses finally came to an end when supporters of Richard III (York) were defeated at the battle of Bosworth Field in 1485 by those of Henry VII (Lancaster), a victory that inspired the reign of the Tudors. To ensure security of the throne for himself and his heirs, in January 1486, Henry VII, Henry Tudor, married Elizabeth of York, the eldest daughter of Edward IV and sister of Edward V, thereby effectively amalgamating the two lines of descent.

In the same year that Henry achieved the throne of England, William Caxton printed Malory's *Morte d'Arthur*. Malory indicated that the city of Winchester had been built on the ruined remains of Camelot. Winchester had been associated with royalty for 700 years and included a fortified castle as a royal residence of which only the Great Hall now remains. So the connection of Winchester with King Alfred, Camelot and royalty were particularly strong when Henry assumed the throne. To add to the intrigue, Henry, his father and grandfather were all of Welsh origin, so the connections of

Arthurian legend with Wales and Winchester, the Grail Romances of old, and the printing of *Morte d'Arthur* must have all been prominent in the royal court at that time. In September 1486, the same year as his marriage to Elizabeth, Henry's first child, a son, was born. As the months of her confinement came to an end, Elizabeth was sent to Winchester, the legendary site of Camelot, for the birth. The child was christened in Winchester Cathedral as Arthur, so named after the legendary king.

Prince Arthur died at the age of 14 in 1502, just four months after a political marriage to a young Spanish princess, Catherine of Aragon. Arthur's premature death left the path of succession open to his brother, who became Henry VIII, and took Catherine as his first wife out of respect for his brother and in order to maintain the political alliance the marriage involved.

The origins of the Round Table on display in Winchester's Great Hall are uncertain, but information available at Winchester states that was made from English oak and is extremely heavy. It may have originally been covered with leather, and to support its weight it had 12 equi-spaced legs close to the outer circumference and a single supporting leg in the centre. These numbers, 12 and 13, are closely associated with symbolism that was common at that time, which we will look at in another section of this book. Tradition has it that the table, as we now see it, may have been embellished with the Arthurian theme in the reign of Henry VIII as a tribute to his late brother. Arthur sits prominently at a clearly defined point to imply the head of the table, whilst the names of knights associated with the Arthurian mythology decorate the outer edge, indicating their position when seated at the table.[25] The centre is dominated by an image of the Tudor rose, the red rose of the House of Lancaster being dominant, surrounding and enclosing the white rose of York.

The Round Table is a symbol strongly associated with King Arthur and a group of knights. The circular aspect of the table may have its own significance that we will come to later. This leaves us with the concept of kings and knights. How did one become a king or a knight?

Section 3

The Making of Kings, Nobles and Knights

There is the long-standing image of a king creating a knight by the laying of a sword blade on each shoulder of the person being raised to this status, a ceremonial process known as 'dubbing'. So where and how did the power of kings evolve? What acts created their right to perform such a ceremony? It is based both on archaic traditions and religious doctrine.

The title 'king' in the English language is a term which in modern times has come to mean the person who is the tribal chief or leader over an entire nation of peoples. Such positions as tribal chief, for example, were historically achieved primarily through eminence as a warrior. Later, some of these leaderships became dynastic, being handed down through family bloodlines, which meant that such positions of authority owed more to accidents of birth than to any demonstrable achievement to the benefit of the people under their rule.

The age of chivalry as so often painted in the imagination, with its knights in shining armour, astride their strutting charger and setting out on quests to do good with lance in hand and banner flying, is very much the image portrayed of a knight from the post-Crusade era. The knights of this era and before the Crusades were mainly products of a political system of rule in Europe known as feudalism. It was a political system best illustrated by what some academics have come to refer to as the pyramid of power. The pyramid of power and concept of the rights of kings are interwoven. The emergence of Orders of Knighthood is interwoven with them.

The Power and Rights of Kings

There have been leaders of peoples for thousands of years. The word 'king' in English is sometimes retrospectively applied to leaders of other nations, where different titles meant broadly the same thing. For instance, the pharaohs of Egypt were essentially kings in their time. Certain biblical tribal leaders have, in translations, been referred to as kings, such as King David or King Solomon. In the Roman Empire, the title Caesar was another word for the position of king as we interpret it today. Throughout history we can see evidence of periods in various societies where kings were elected by the citizens over whom they would exercise authority, and other periods when they became dynastic.

Many of the traditions of kingship in Western Europe have descended and been modified from the practices of the Roman Empire and its aftermath. According to historians, in the early period of the Roman kingdom, kings were elected by the people, and served in that capacity for the period of their life. At the death of one king, the people would elect a new king. Later, a hereditary process evolved where the right of kingship flowed through the female line of a deceased king. From the earliest days of the formation of Rome by Romulus, the Senate had been the centre of power with Senators having been selected from the 300 most noble and legitimate families. It became the prerogative of the king to select those who would serve in the Senate. At this stage in the development of early Rome, the role of the king was considered as being akin to that of a chief executive, acting on behalf of, and in concert with, the Senate. This changed to a system of monarchy in which the king became the supreme authority over military, civil, judicial and religious matters and the Senators became advisors to the king, although new laws required the approval of the Senate.

When a king died, the Senate would seek and propose another person to that role. The person selected would be paraded before the people, who would either confirm the choice of the Senators or reject it. If selected, he would pass through a ceremony of investiture which included seeking the approval of the gods. Only when such formalities were completed did the new king assume power. Thus we see in this process the candidate being selected by the nobles and acceptance being gained from the people, with the perceived divine approval of the gods. It is very similar to the practices adopted by later tribes such as the Carolingians following the collapse of Rome in the 5th century, whereby the nobles selected the king as supreme warrior and raised him up above their heads on a shield for all to see. It is in the latter stages of the Roman Empire that we observe the role of Emperor assuming absolute power, as with some kingships after the 8th century.

In Europe the rise of Christianity brought with it another parallel layer of hierarchy that had been introduced from the time of Constantine and the Council of Nicaea, the hierarchy of the church itself, with its archbishops and bishops at the head, and the priests at the lower levels. The kings reported to the Emperor, so the bishops reported to the Pope. Bishops also had influence in territorial governance, took legal jurisdiction in numerous matters, and even had their own prison system. Kings looked after civil order; bishops looked after spiritual matters. Kings had palaces; bishops had palaces. Kings had land under their control as a means of securing the boundaries of the kingdom. Bishops had land under their control, land that was often passed to their control and that of the Church in anticipation that the giver would be well received when their day of judgement finally arrived. In consequence there was effectively a two-tier system of governance. It was a system that provoked much debate as to which line of authority really had the controlling power – the kings or the bishops.

When the Emperor Constantine used the Christian religion as a way of unifying the Roman Empire, he appointed the Pope of that time. When the Roman Church effectively broke away from the Byzantine Roman Empire and anointed Charlemagne as Emperor, it also provided for the Emperor to appoint the next Pope when that position became vacant.[26] The Pope would then anoint and crown the next Emperor when, likewise, that position became vacant. As a consequence of this process there then existed two pyramids of power. In the one pyramid the principal position was that of the Emperor, and kings were subservient to the Emperor. This pyramid was primarily responsible for all secular matters. In the other pyramid the Pope was at the principal position and governed all religious matters. So within the hierarchical structure of Western

Europe, the Emperor appointed the Pope; the Pope would crown the next Emperor; kings were subservient to the Emperor; archbishops and bishops would report to the Pope; and the bishops would anoint and crown the kings.

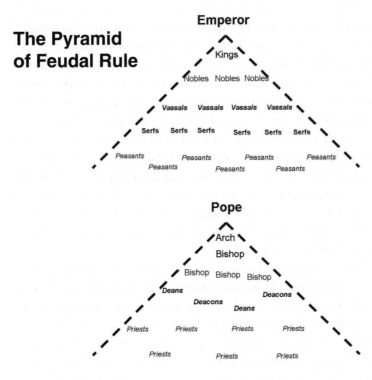

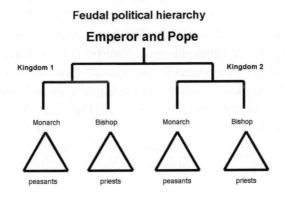

Feudal political hierarchy

This system of hierarchical structure became known as the feudal system of the Middle Ages. In this structure the Emperor was the secular head of the Empire, and being a warrior, had a primary role in providing military protection for the Church.

As noted in an earlier section, the bishops held considerable power over the earlier Christian Roman Emperors and could become involved in the settlement of disputes and legal issues. They even decided what literature people could read – a form of state-endorsed censorship. In addition to their spiritual role, many bishops became part of the nobility and played a role in the administration of state affairs. This is not perhaps surprising. The universal language of state and religion across Europe was Latin. Many nobles and kings could neither read nor write, so the bishops and clergy, who had such abilities, were obviously in demand. With wealthy landowners offering land to the Church in the hope of eternal salvation as a reward, some such bishops became very wealthy, with their income inflated from considerable holdings of land attached to their office.

In addition, the Church through its bishops received tithes. This was an expectation that everyone contributed ten per cent of their income to the Church as a means of paying for its administration. With most of the people in the feudal system working on the land, much of that payment was in agricultural produce. The precedent for this payment came from the Old Testament. Although it was considered to be a voluntary contribution, in the Middle Ages it was often treated as an enforced tax for the benefit of the Church. Such taxes/tithes only added yet further to the wealth of the bishops.

Over the next few hundred years following the passing of Charlemagne, it became common practice for the office of bishop of the Church to be purchased from the king or other senior nobles. This was deemed as simony, namely the deliberate buying or selling of anything with a spiritual connection. The Catholic Encyclopedia defines this as follows:

> '*Simony is usually defined "a deliberate intention of buying or selling for a temporal price such things as are spiritual of annexed unto*

spirituals". While this definition only speaks of purchase and sale, any exchange of spiritual for temporal things is simoniacal. Nor is the giving of the temporal as the price of the spiritual required for the existence of simony; … it suffices that the determining motive of the action of one party be the obtaining of compensation from the other.[27]

By the practice of buying the office, such bishops were in effect purchasing the right to anoint and crown kings. This was an unsavoury practice that led to what has become known as the Investiture Controversy in the 11th century, which was a dispute between the Holy Roman Emperor, Henry IV and Pope Gregory VII as to who had authority over the appointment of church officials, such as bishops, in kingdoms. Was it the king who ruled his kingdom, and thereby both secular and spiritual affairs, or the Pope who ruled over the Church of Rome, and thereby spiritual matters? This contentious issue was resolved in 1056 CE when a gathering in Rome of Church officials removed the right of emperors, and thereby secular authorities, to appoint Popes, insisting that this could only be done by officials of the Church. To do this they created the College of Cardinals as the selection body, a process that is still current 1,000 years later in the 21st century.

Thus there was a concept that the Church of Rome had been founded by God, and that the Pope was therefore the spiritual representative of the deity and had universal power. Kings were anointed and crowned by bishops who were appointed under papal authority and therefore viewed as having been *divinely* selected and conferred in office. Therefore it could be said that kings and their descendants were chosen by the deity, and as such had a divine right to rule in all secular matters irrespective of the wishes of the people, nobility or other functionaries within the kingdom. It became the founding principle for the legitimacy of monarchs to rule by absolute power from the medieval period through to that of modern European history. Through that power and the philosophy attached to the office of ruler, it was deemed that the king had the right to appoint nobles and knights alike, or to delegate such power if the circumstances were appropriate.

From the time of Charlemagne, the ceremony and anointment of kings took place with the king sitting in a regal chair which we have come to know as a throne. Not so, however, in Scotland. Whereas in the Holy Roman Empire the position of king was deemed a divine appointment, in Scotland the king was chosen by the clan chiefs. His coronation was affirmed by him sitting and standing on a particular stone, which became known as the Stone of Destiny or Stone of Scone. According to legend, this one stone had been used for the acclamation of Scottish kings from around 850 until 1292 CE when it was captured by Edward I of England, removed from Scotland and built into a special throne, known as St Edward's Chair that was subsequently placed in Westminster Abbey. A further legend counterclaims Edward's prize by suggesting that what Edward took away was a replica and the real stone had been hidden. In removing the stone, Edward was affirming his conquest of Scotland because, in theory, without the stone there could be no legitimate claims to kingship in Scotland.

The history surrounding the creation of the kings of Scotland is a subject in its own right. What is of note here is the similarity to the kingship process that existed in the time of Pepin, for example, when the tribal chief or warrior was selected and acclaimed by his peers and stood on a shield to be raised above the assembled chiefs as an indication that he now served/ruled over them, as mentioned earlier. The kings of Scotland were selected by the tribal chiefs and by standing on the stone would have been raised above them.

Before leaving the Stone of Scone, there is one small historical note that is never mentioned in general school education. Having installed the Stone of Scone in Westminster Abbey, every subsequent King of England sat on, or just above, the supposed stone, implying that coronation as Kings of England was also mastery over Scotland. During the centuries that followed there was a great deal of skirmishing between the two countries: by Scotland in the interests of establishing and maintaining its independence, and by England in attempting to subjugate the Scots.

In 1707, the Act of Union between England and Scotland created a new realm, the Kingdom of Great Britain, and its first monarch was Queen Anne. When Charles II died in 1685 he had left no legitimate heirs, so the throne of England had passed to his brother James. James was Anne's father and a devout Roman Catholic. As a Catholic he could not hold the throne of England, so he and his wife were forced into exile in 1689. The throne then passed to Anne's brother-in-law and sister, William and Mary, who ruled as joint monarchs, the only time such an arrangement has been permitted. Mary died in 1694 leaving William to then rule as sole monarch. He died in 1702 at which time the throne passed to Anne. The Act of Union took place five years into her reign. At that time Ireland was also under English dominance. Thus the titles Anne inherited were Queen of Great Britain, Queen of Ireland and Queen of France. The title 'King/Queen of France' was claimed by English and British monarchs from 1340 until 1801, despite the fact that, with the exception of what we know as the Channel Islands, English dominance over former territories in northern France had ceased to exist from around 1560. The claim was dropped with the creation of another state in 1801, the United Kingdom of Great Britain and Ireland, subsequently re-titled as the United Kingdom of Great Britain and Northern Ireland following the creation of the Irish Republic in the 20th century.

Setting aside the appointment of the kings of Scotland, the concept that the king was perceived to have been divinely selected, that his decisions were divinely guided, and as such he had a divine right to rule, prevailed in much of Western Europe from around 800 to about 1450 CE when a different spiritual force came to the fore – Protestantism. From around that time and for the next 200 years a series of events challenged the views and traditions of the Roman Church and the supremacy of the Pope and Emperor. There had been several attempts to translate the Holy Bible from Latin, which was the language of the church, into the local languages of the people of the various countries that constituted the Holy Roman Empire. Such translations were considered to be in the vulgar language and resulted in many well-educated men being murdered by the Church in an attempt to prevent such translations from being produced. Needless to say, in authorising such murders the Church was sending a message warning others who might try to walk a similar path not to do so.

Martin Luther, a well-connected and prominent character in the Roman Catholic faith, became a driver for change in the 16th century and created what has become known as the Great Religious Revolt. It resulted in a series of religious wars across the Holy Roman Empire as Protestants sought to throw off the trappings of indulgencies and imagery used in Roman Catholicism. It resulted in whole countries denying the Catholic faith and, as such, their part in the Empire. Amongst these was the English king, Henry VIII. In his younger days he had been a strong advocate of the Roman Church and respectful of the role of the Emperor. Henry had written a book extolling the virtues of the Catholic faith and denouncing the views of Martin Luther, even sending a copy of the book to the Pope.

Henry had married Catherine of Aragon, the wife of his older brother, after Prince Arthur had died at a young age. Henry was a deeply religious man and came to believe that his marriage to Catherine had been unlawful and that he had committed a sin by living with her. He had fallen in love with a young lady, Anne Boleyn, but was denied the prospect of a divorce from his wife, Catherine, by the Pope. Henry used Parliament as a means of bringing about changes in his favour. In particular, Parliament passed a series of acts that progressively diminished papal influence over the kingdom and the value of revenues that the monasteries and Church received. A young man, Thomas Cranmer, found favour with the king. He suggested that as the Doctors of Divinity at the universities, then based at Oxford and Cambridge, were well acquainted with the text of the Bible, they should be used to pass judgement as to whether or not a divorce or annulment of the marriage to Catherine was possible on religious grounds. Henry appointed Cranmer as Archbishop of Canterbury, a position confirmed by the Pope. The Doctors of Divinity ruled in favour of the annulment of the marriage to Catherine, and Cranmer therefore declared the marriage invalid, a pronouncement which irritated the Vatican. Henry then used Parliament to proclaim himself Supreme Head of the Church of England, married Anne Boleyn and made her Queen. The Vatican responded by excommunicating Henry. Further Acts of Parliament were passed declaring that England was an empire in its own right and that the king was its sole head and authority. With this Act of Parliament, Henry had withdrawn the country from the Holy Roman Empire and in so doing, removed himself from loyalty to the Emperor and the authority of the Pope. After 700 years, it meant that Rome no longer had any legislative, appellate or religious influence on the affairs of England. It was an act that threatened to destabilise the Holy Roman Empire.

Henry realised that with the numerous abbeys, convents and monasteries that existed in England, all promulgating and operating within the context of the Catholic faith, there was the potential for an undercurrent of dissent that could threaten the throne. In addition, their revenues had in some cases also enhanced the financial capability of elements of the nobility who might support a reconnection with Rome. The monasteries were progressively abolished and their treasures and items of value transferred to the king. Thus Henry took unto himself as the King of England to be the head of religious and secular matters, subservient to no other external power. By the declaration that England was an empire unto itself, Henry was effectively proclaiming himself as an emperor. Having previously been declared Defender of the Faith of the Church of England, he was now the spiritual head of the new English empire. This was the English Reformation. The King of England no longer needed to rely on the service of knighthoods constituted elsewhere in the Roman Empire but could institute his own.

Despite the growth of Protestantism in a number of states of Europe, the Holy Roman Empire and the position of the Emperor within it continued to exist until 1806. Two years earlier in May 1804, Napoleon had declared the existence of the French Empire, having won a series of territorial battles across Europe. The declaration was followed later in the year when a ceremony was held at the cathedral of Notre Dame in Paris. On 2 December 1804, Napoleon placed the crown on his own head, declared himself Emperor and crowned his wife Josephine as Empress. The Pope was in attendance but took no part in the ceremony, which would otherwise have endorsed the authority of the new Emperor. Historians generally attribute these acts of Napoleon as an attempt to imitate the Emperor Charlemagne 1,000 years previously.

The empire created by Charlemagne had been in steady decline for hundreds of years prior to arrival on the scene of Napoleon. The last Emperor to have been crowned by a Pope had been in 1440 CE, after which the title remained in the province of the Habsburgs for some 300 years. The extent of the Holy Roman Empire, and thereby the influence extended by its Emperor, was diminished following a series of battles led by Napoleon Bonaparte that resulted in victory for the growing French Empire that he commanded. These territories were then secured by Napoleon appointing the rulers of captured states. Their allegiance was to the Emperor of France and not to the Holy Roman Emperor. Thus the extent of the Holy Roman Empire was greatly diminished.

The Holy Roman Empire was dissolved by the last Emperor, Francis II, in August 1806 following an ultimatum from Napoleon, who by that time had conquered much of Western Europe, the island of Malta and swathes of North Africa, including Egypt. A month prior to the dissolution of the Holy Roman Empire, Napoleon had created the Confederation of the Rhine. Sixteen small German States, their security guaranteed by Napoleon as their protector, formally left the Holy Roman Empire to form the new Confederation. They were progressively joined by many more, so that at its zenith the Confederation comprised around 40 such states. The Confederation of the Rhine had a short life and ended after the ill-fated attempt by Napoleon to conquer Russia in 1813. A series of other battles in Germany left Napoleon's army considerably weakened in precursors to the Battle of Waterloo. During this period many of the German states that had been members of the

Confederation left and changed allegiance. In 1815, following the defeat and capture of Napoleon, the map of Europe was again redrawn and a German Confederation created whose borders closely matched that of the former Confederation of the Rhine.

What is significant, however, is that in the formation of the Confederation of the Rhine, all Orders of Knighthood that existed in that territory were withdrawn, with the exception of just two: the Order of St John of Jerusalem and the Order of the Teutonic Knights.

Notwithstanding the title of Holy Roman Emperor being retained by the Habsburgs, which implied that only they were divinely chosen, the rise of Protestantism and the break with the Roman Church, or the abolition of the Holy Roman Empire by Napoleon, monarchs throughout Western Europe have in many cases continued to claim a 'right to rule'. It is a right based on the chance created by an accident of birth rather than the acclamation or approval of the citizens of their country.

The Influence of the Nobles
Man by his nature is not a being who lives easily in isolation – he lives in groups that vary in size, and each group is a society in its own right. Where there is a society of beings, it is natural that there will be individuals of outstanding physical or intellectual ability who will rise above the rest and become leaders.

In former times, 7,000 years ago, there were no kings. There were merely tribal leaders. The leader would demonstrate allegiance to the people of his tribe, whilst the tribe would be expected to show allegiance to the leader. In some eras of the ancient world the leader, once elected or accepted, would be raised to the status of a god and in many cases retain that status for life. Having secured the leadership role, sometimes by a process of election by the elders of a tribe, sometimes through brute force, the leader needed protection against both external invaders and usurpers within his own tribe. From this protected position leaders could exercise absolute power; they were in total control, subservient to nobody, until they were defeated.

Men who distinguished themselves in battle in support of the leader would often be rewarded by sharing the spoils and riches associated with a conquest. This in turn provided these warriors with a degree of relative wealth, power and position within the tribe. Later, a leader who had secured a substantial territory would allocate large areas of land to distinguished warriors to both secure the outer boundaries of the territory and provide a sub-rule over groups of people within the tribal area so as to ensure order and reduce the risk of threat within the tribal lands. It was these sub-rulers and their families who then became the nobility and the lands they controlled collectively became countries.

Above all else, in the Middle Ages a king was a warrior. A king like the Emperor Charlemagne may have had an extensive territory to manage and it would have been difficult to do this effectively on his own. Historically, there had been battles between various tribes in various regions of Western Europe as warlords endeavoured to win supremacy over their neighbours and thereby gain in territorial conquest. This was not a satisfactory prospect to be tolerated in any kingdom, not least for the reason that a possible usurper might prove stronger than the ruling king and seize the throne of that country. Maintaining the rule of law was therefore an essential component of kingship and an ability to retain one's throne. To maintain control of his realm the king would appoint a series of nobles or lords who were allocated an area of the kingdom to administer. They were usually selected as being individuals who had served the king well in battle. Some nobles may well have been members of the family of the king and as such the king could usually expect a high degree of allegiance. Such nobles effectively had control over a large area of land, often called a fief – hence the term fiefdom – and were, in effect, sub-kings. Such land was loaned, not given to the noble under a title of ownership, and as such it was their responsibility to maintain and improve the land under their control. In return for their position of power, nobles swore oaths of loyalty to their monarch, provided themselves for military service in support of the king, raised taxes and supplied armies and provisions for the royal household. The noble would also be responsible for supplying the arms and armour that his fighting force may have needed to ensure their effectiveness.

The noble, sometimes referred to by such titles as a lord or baron, would then subdivide his land and loan it to a number of vassals. A vassal was created by the lord through a ceremony by which the individual would be formally installed in his new social position. The ceremony was a way of demonstrating to others in the kingdom that such a status had been conferred and involved swearing oaths of allegiance to his lord, including being prepared to undertake military service. It was then followed by an agreement on what dues/taxes the vassal may have been expected to pay to the lord, and when such dues were to be paid, depending on the area of land loaned to the vassal and the nature of its produce. Thus a lord would usually have several vassals within his domain, all maintaining land, providing services and producing dues/taxes. Nobles thereby became wealthy administrators without the need for endless years of physical toil.

It became common practice that in a dynastic relationship, the title and rights associated with nobility would pass to the eldest surviving son of a noble that died. Of course, a noble may well have had several sons and there was only one noble position to be held. Other sons may well therefore have been made vassals. It is from this group of individuals that many of the later horse-mounted warriors would be selected and become knights. They benefited from their connections with nobility, had income from the land they controlled and, perhaps most importantly, had a need to make their way in the world and perhaps achieve the same level of respect and authority their older siblings had achieved by the accident of birth that made them the eldest son.

A vassal may well have had a sufficiently large area of land such that he could subdivide into a series of lots that he would rent to serfs within his sphere of influence. They in turn would pledge their loyalty to the vassal, who was now effectively their lord, and also agree to provide support, military service and dues/taxes. Thus the vassal accrued wealth and power at a lower level than that of the nobles.

At the bottom of the social strata were the peasants who were the poorest and most hardworking citizens, spending long hours every day maintaining the land, growing crops, tending to livestock and providing services to their masters. Their lives were ruled by the seasons and the type of work that needed to be done in each. In some instances, serfs and peasants were one and the same.

The peasants did most of the work and produced the wealth for their masters, the serfs. A portion of the goods or services accumulated by the serfs was passed on to the vassals as dues. From the total of the dues collected by the vassals, a portion was passed on to the nobles. From the total of the dues collected by the nobles, a portion was passed on to the king.

During the period prior to the Crusades it was from the social layer of vassals who pledged loyalty to the nobles that the elite mounted warriors, later to be associated with knights, would usually be recruited. Through their efforts and loyalty, perhaps they would become nobles themselves. Until the 11th century there were very few organisations that could be regarded as specific Orders of Knighthood. That changed, however, when certain groups of nobles and vassals came together against a background of the threat to key sites of religious significance, which led to the Crusades. It is then that we find the establishment of Orders of Knighthood, underwritten by the religious authority, that have formed the basis of our perceptions of chivalry. The mounted warriors on horseback, clad in metal armour, banners flying high and with sword in hand, became fashionable. Nobles themselves wanted to be regarded as knights, to be seen as brave and entering service on behalf of their religion. It became a vehicle for winning and enhancing the respect they demanded from their underlings together with power and influence within the kingdom. And just as noble hereditary titles became the domain of the ruling elite, so they began to acquire similar hereditary status within Orders of Knighthood. Knights were no longer chosen from mere vassals, but from within the nobility itself.

Arise Sir Knight – and take a bath

A knight was a warrior – not necessarily with a title to any land – a mounted soldier, well trained and armed. By the medieval period, the knights were the cavalry, mounting attacks on an enemy, on horseback.

Various records show that the French equivalent of the English word 'knight' was *Chevalier;* the equivalent in German was *Ritter;* the Spanish *Caballero;* and in Poland it was *Rycerz.* All these titles meant the same thing: a horse rider. It is only in the English language, it seems, that the word 'knight' came to create a distinctive title in its own right and a platform for lower orders of nobility.

After the early 14th century, when the Crusades had come to an end and the continuation of religious Orders of Knighthood seemed irrelevant, kings throughout Europe created their own Orders of Knighthood, inspired by what they perceived the role of knight had been. In the era of the Crusades, several kings – like Richard the Lionheart – had gone into battle in the Holy Land. By around the year 1320, however, the only connection with that era would have been the stories that were handed down, some of which undoubtedly became myths and legends, and found their way into the poetry of the times. This stream of poetry is usually referred to as the Romances. It is around this time that stories of King Arthur and the Knights of the Round Table came to the fore with the publication of Malory's *Morte d'Arthur.* A whole new image of the knight gradually took shape – a charismatic, trustworthy, loyal, fearless warrior and a champion of honourable causes.

So how was a knight made a knight?

For hundreds if not thousands of years almost every culture in the world had small groups of individuals as bodyguards for its chief, or an elite fighting force. It is evident from the tribes of Africa to the remote civilisations of South America. There had to be some means by which they were proven worthy of such important status before they achieved that recognition. In almost all cases the accolade was based on some form of battlefield honour. This might have been the award of a plume of feathers that adorned a headdress, with the feathers being given for each battle in which the individual had taken part. In another society the qualifying test may have been to kill a lion with a bow and arrow. Ashmole notes a particular practice from South America, as follows:

> 'The… Lords of Peru dedicated their children to Honour… They pierced their ears, whipped them with slings, smeared their faces with blood in order they be true knights…Those of Royal extraction before they received the Order of Knighthood, abstained for seven days from all manner of nutriment, except a little raw grain and water, and after being heartened and brisked up again, performed some military exercises, also racing, wrestling, leaping, shooting, slinging, throwing the dart and lance, etc., and enduring to be beaten on the hands and legs with wands; these being as it were the tests where they could endure the hardships of war or no; for if they did not endure them manfully, they were denied knighthood.'[28]

There are records that state that in the late Middle Ages, during the coronation of the King of the Romans and the Holy Roman Emperor, special ceremonies were held where several individuals received the accolade of being made knights.[29] This implies that they were not nobles who might otherwise have inherited such a title. It also suggests that the King/Emperor was rewarding individuals deemed worthy of recognition for some service already undertaken who might otherwise not have been honoured.

Not all knights received that honour at the hands of kings or emperors, nor were elaborate ceremonies organised for the purpose. According to the Catholic Encyclopedia, the primary requirements of becoming a knight were birth, age and training. Birth meant that the individual was from a recognised noble family. As such, from early boyhood the individual would have been sent to special weapons training schools and taught horsemanship and the care of the animals. Beyond that he would be sent to serve in the house or castle of another noble family where, in serving the master of the house, he would learn civility, manners and courtesy. To be of age usually meant having reached the age of 21 years.

Assuming the three primary characteristics could be met, an existing knight had the authority to confer a knighthood on others. Hence a young man who had been in the service of a lord who was himself a knight may well have been knighted by that lord. However, if the condition of birth could not be met, then the king alone had the authority to confer knighthoods.[30] By virtue that Holy Roman Emperors are recorded as making knights at their coronation, it would imply that amongst those being so honoured may well have been deserving individuals who were not from families deemed to be noble. This did not prevent a person who met the criteria for knighthood from being ceremonially conferred by the king. There is evidence that some individuals who could have chosen to have the accolade conferred on them by the king nevertheless chose to receive their knighthoods from the hands of other knights whom they admired and held in high esteem.

The full ceremony of receiving the knighthood was in reality the end of a ritualistic process. There are several historical documents that show there was an elaborate process of preparation for those who were to receive this accolade, and that the entire process contained discreet symbolism. In many cases, depending on the type of Order one was being admitted to, the process was not without some enormous cost to the recipient.

Invariably the proposed recipient would be required to attend a place of ceremony and would therefore arrive in clothes of their choice. It may well have been that the recipient had travelled many miles on horseback for several days without a change of clothes. The era of the Middle Ages was not known for its habitual washing and superior toiletry practices of the populace at large. Shaving may also have been difficult, so the candidate would boast a bushy beard containing evidence of meals eaten days before. Neither was there routine hair care, so hair could be long, matted and home to a range of crawling insects. It would have been entirely discourteous for the prospective recipient to have been presented to a king and his court for an important ceremonial occasion in such a state, unless of course the honour was being awarded directly on a battlefield after an arduous day of fighting. Thus the pre-process was something of a ritual, attended no doubt by other knights who were aware of the process and the symbolism attached to it and would guide the candidate through the various elements of preparation. It seems the ritual began with a thorough brushing out of hair, no doubt having it cut and trimmed into some order deemed acceptable.

Next came a bath. The clothes that were removed were apparently regarded as inappropriate for the future knight and as such were given to an attendant as a gift for services provided. We must remember that during this time the prevailing religion across Europe was Christianity, so it seems that bathing as part of the ritual preparation was not just a process of cleaning a body of dirt and odour but also served as a form of baptism and ritualised purification. The symbolic consequence of washing the candidate was that he was deemed to emerge from it clean and free from sin.

Having bathed, the candidate was then led to a bed to rest. As he lay on the bed he was encouraged to contemplate that at the end of his life he would be interred in that position and therefore for the rest of his life he should devote his energies to service, avoid involvement in conspiracies or acts of treason, be charitable and generous to others and a protector of maidens, so that he might ultimately be delivered before his maker as having served a good and righteous life. To remind him of this he would later be dressed in brown stockings to symbolise the earth in which he would ultimately be buried.

Following this period of reflection the candidate was then raised from the bed and dressed in a white cloth or robe signifying purity and cleanliness, as in Christianity these attributes are deemed to be derived from baptism. The prospective knight was then clothed in a scarlet robe to symbolise that he may be called on to shed blood in defence of the Church. Around his waist would be a white belt that symbolised purity and chastity as a reminder that he should not give way to lust and lechery and the resulting temptations that might be placed in his path.

He was then adorned with golden spurs. The Old Testament contains what are known as the Ten Commandments which Moses is credited with having received directly from God. They are a code of conduct for a civilised community. Thus the knight was being reminded that he should move forward with vigour, and live by and promote the code of conduct expressed through the Commandments, in the same way that a horse would press forward when urged on by the use of the spurs.

The last items with which he would be provided were a scabbard and sword. The sword has two sharp edges and in the process of dubbing, namely the placing of the flat side of the blade of the sword on each shoulder of the candidate, one edge is directed towards the candidate whilst the other is pointing to the wider world. As such the two outer edges are first to remind the candidate to seek truth and cut through obstacles that prevent truth from being revealed, and second to ensure justice to the benefit of the realm. The sword when placed in the scabbard is benign and as such symbolises mercy.[31]

Throughout the ceremony there would have been an explanation of the symbolic meaning of the various items of adornment. At specific stages there would also have been a need for a declaration of obedience and fealty to the king or lord.

Depending on the Order of Knighthood, a coat of arms may also have been presented to the new knight. This coat of arms would have been represented on a banner, so that when on the battlefield it would be seen by all that the knight was performing the service and loyalty that he had sworn to provide by putting his life on the line and fighting to protect the Church, the king and realm.

All of the above symbolic elements, or the rituals, are at the core of the concept of chivalry.

Prior to being finally conferred a knight, the recipient may have had to give away other possessions, including his horse, as with his clothes at the time of bathing. This was to symbolise that having been made a knight he was leaving behind his old ways and having been cleansed and symbolically baptised, his renewed life should be directed in the paths of chivalry.

As discussed earlier, Orders of Knighthood as we have come to know them do not seem to appear as such until the 11th century. The ritual of the making of a knight, as described above, is based primarily on information that seems to be derived from the 13th century. Although reference is made earlier to Holy Roman Emperors who made knights as part of their coronation, we are referring primarily to the Germanic emperors such as Charles IV. He lived from 1316 to 1378, and became Emperor in 1355.[32] This is an era – the late Middle Ages – that later came to define the concepts of chivalry.

Throughout the above description of the ritual associated with making a knight no mention has been made of the Church or that any of its ministers played any part in the ceremony. However, keeping in mind the role of religion in society at that time, no doubt prayers were said at some stage in the proceedings or there was some other special intervention by a bishop or senior cleric attached to the Church.

At the time of the Crusades, long before emperors like Charles IV, the Church did take upon itself a ritual process of making knights. The ritual was very similar to that which has been described above, except that it also required periods of vigil and contemplation in a church.[33] Perhaps the Church therefore provided the template for the form of knighthood from the late Middle Ages that came to provide the image of chivalry as we now know it. And it started in the late 11th century.

The Spiritual Knights

Jerusalem, a small village which developed into a city, has known little by way of peace in its 3500 years of history. It is the location of Mount Moriah where, according to biblical tradition, Abraham was to take his son Isaac for sacrifice. It was the town that David made his capital; it was, again according to biblical tradition, the place where the Israelites built the first Jewish temple – Solomon's Temple – and where the events that inspired the Christian religion 2,000 years ago took place. When the Western Roman Empire collapsed,

Jerusalem entered a period of relative peace when the followers of the main religions of Islam, Judaism and Christianity lived side by side without too much difficulty under the rule of the Roman Byzantine Empire based in Constantinople. Jerusalem was a city of pilgrimage for the devout Christians of Europe and the Muslims of the Middle East. Then, in the 11th century, the city and what had by that time become known as the Holy Land was invaded and fell again, this time to an army sometimes referred to as Seljuk Turks who were supporters of the Islamic religion. According to historians, this invading army originated in an area of Kazakhstan near the Caspian Sea and grew to prominence in the late 10th and early 11th centuries.

It seems that the Seljuks may originally have descended from Jewish or Christian ancestry, but then converted to Islam. By the mid-11th century, their army had captured much of the territory in what today we know as Iran, Iraq and Syria, subduing Baghdad in the process. In 1071, the Seljuks battled successfully against the Byzantine army led by Alexios I, after which they moved on to the Holy Land. They also conquered much of Persia to found what became known as the Great Seljuk Empire. The Seljuks continued to make inroads on Byzantine territory until Alexios I wrote to Pope Urban II seeking his support in providing an army to defend Byzantium. As mentioned earlier, the Roman Byzantine Empire descended from the Roman Empire of the East, and it was in the reign of Charlemagne that the Roman Church separated from Byzantium to form what we know as Western Europe; some historians note that Urban II's agreement to support Alexios may have had as much to do with seeking a reunification of the Empire as it did in simply providing aid to stop the Seljuks.

Having taken the Holy Land, the Seljuks prevented Christians from making pilgrimages to what they regarded as a sacred city. Thus it was that the two concerns about the survival of Byzantium and the denial of access to Jerusalem resulted in Pope Urban II summoning a council at Clermont in France in November 1095. Some 225 bishops and nearly 100 abbots from across Europe were in attendance.[34] Thousands of noblemen were also present. All agreed that an army should be sent to Jerusalem to free it from the control of the invaders. The Crusades were initiated and Jerusalem fell to the crusader army on 15 July 1099.

It is around the period of the First Crusade that we see the emergence of spiritual or religious knights. Foremost amongst these was the Order of St John of Jerusalem, the Order of the Poor Soldiers of Christ and the Temple of Solomon, and the Teutonic Knights.

To Summarise

From the above we note that the kings derived their power from the Church. The nobles derived their positions in society from the kings. Knights derived their accolades from other knights assuming the candidate was of noble birth or from kings if the candidate for knighthood could not prove noble birth.

The invasion of the Holy Land and threat to the Byzantine Empire was the basis for what has become known as the First Crusade.

It is highly likely that those we have come to see through popular imagery as being knights in the late Middle Ages would, in earlier times, have been the horsemen that made up the armoured cavalry in armies in the period ranging from the end of the Western Roman Empire through the era of Charlemagne and until the arrival of the more secular Orders that were created during and after the 14th century.

Throughout the ritual of being made a knight, the ceremonial trappings held great symbolism. It is that symbolism that we later find as the concept behind the single word 'chivalry'.

Section 4

The Major Orders of Knighthood

The word 'order' has many definitions in the English language. One such meaning is a monastic organisation. It is from this definition that the term became associated with knights and chivalry. In simple terms, monastic orders are groups of people who have felt a need to devote their lives to serving God, in whichever form they determine the deity to be. Such men are referred to as monks, and their female equivalents are known as nuns. The word 'monk' is derived from the Latin *monachus* which means 'religious hermit'. The female equivalent in Latin is *nonna* which is translated as 'tutor'. Irrespective of these definitions, within the Orders they were brothers and sisters. One other term associated with monastic life is the word 'friar'. Although widely used to define the same role as a monk, friars were in fact members of what became known as mendicant orders. These were essentially the same as any other monastic order, but derived their income and lifestyle from begging and relying on the charity and generosity that others showed to them. There are several denominations to which Orders might be attached: the Roman Catholic, Anglican and Greek Orthodox churches are examples. Each of the Orders has followed a general rule of conduct, such as the Rule of Benedict, the Rule of St Basil and the Rule of St Augustine.

In Europe in the Middle Ages these Orders did not operate and reside in one location; they had many houses spread over the entire continent. The Cistercians, for example, had around 15 major centres in Britain alone, in addition to smaller houses. The nature of the Order dictated their primary outlook. The Benedictines were strict and their beliefs demanded a life that involved poverty, chastity and hard physical work. The Augustinians had strict rules of obedience and were renowned for their charity and hospitality. It seems that the Augustinians were therefore popular with the community at large.

Some of the monasteries were in isolated communities and for safety and defence their enclaves resembled fortresses. In southern Europe, the worlds of Christianity and Islam often collided. Islamic forces occupied much of what today we know as Portugal, Spain and southern France. If areas of land were not controlled by Islamic invaders, such as Provence in southern France, they may have been subjected to regular raids by invading groups. It therefore became a feature of monastic life in such threatened areas that monks were well armed out of necessity to defend their monasteries, and defend them they did. Although committed to God's service, they could be powerful brothers-in-arms.

Throughout the Middle Ages, Europe was dominated by the single Roman Catholic religion; there was a perception that kings were selected for their roles by God and therefore kings created knights from men who were born and brought up in a culture that worshipped God. Hence it is not surprising that many of the later organisations that signified knights became known as Orders.

Today they are usually defined as being in one of two groups:

- monastic orders
- military orders.

From the start of the era of the Crusades in the late 11th century, nearly all Orders of Knighthood have been of the military variety. One of the first such to be established was in Jerusalem.

Jerusalem before the Crusades

Jerusalem is one of the oldest surviving cities in the world with a history that goes back at least six centuries, having been founded originally around 4000 BCE. The Old Testament informs us that it was the City of David, the place he forged as the centre of the Hebrew world and where his son Solomon built the first Hebrew temple. It is a city that has been recorded as having been invaded by the Egyptians, Babylonians, Persians, Assyrians, Greeks, Romans and Arabs.

By the mid-6th century, the Roman Empire was centred on Constantinople, and the resultant Byzantine Empire controlled much of the Levant bordering the eastern Mediterranean, including the Holy Land and Syria.

In the later years of what today we call the era BC (before Christ) or BCE (before the Common Era), a period that started some 2,000 years ago and extends back into ancient history, King Herod ruled Judaea from Jerusalem as a satellite state of the Roman Empire. In the early years of the Common Era, Rome took direct administrative control of Jerusalem and the surrounding territories. From 66 CE, there was a series of Jewish uprisings against Roman rule. This resulted in the Jewish armies being defeated at Masada in 70 CE, following which the Herodian Jewish Temple built on the site occupied by Solomon's Temple 1,000 years earlier was destroyed by the Romans. The temple was the centre of power and influence in Jewish life, so having destroyed it the Romans banned the Jews from rebuilding it.

Although the Jews were defeated at Masada, it did not stop wars and rebellions against Roman authority. Between each conflict the Jews returned to Jerusalem for short periods and areas of the city were rebuilt. Principal amongst these rebellions was the Bar Kokhba revolt in 132 CE. This was the last major Jewish revolt against Roman rule and resulted in the re-establishment of Jewish control over not just Jerusalem but the whole of Judaea. It was a revolt that saw massive losses on the part of the Roman legions. Historians estimate that about 600,000 Jews were killed in this uprising alone. The Bar Kokhba victory was short lived. After three years of fighting, Jerusalem was recaptured by Emperor Hadrian in 135 CE. Hadrian renamed it *Aelia Capitolina*. By this stage revolts against the Romans had been ongoing for around 70 years. To ensure the Jews could not stage another uprising Hadrian persecuted them, destroyed many of their major towns and villages across Judaea and banned them from entering the city so that it could no longer be a focus of their lives, customs and religion. The ban continued for almost 500 years.

As mentioned previously, the establishment of the Christian religion as a unifying force in the Roman Empire was conceived by the Emperor Constantine through the Council of Nicaea in 325 CE. It was around this time that Constantine identified or defined a number of what have become Christian sacred sites, including the construction of the Holy Sepulchre in Jerusalem. Jerusalem remained a city ruled by Byzantine Emperors until around 615 CE when it fell to an invading force from Persia, but 15 years later it was back in Roman Byzantine hands. This period of Byzantine control was short lived. The start of the 7th century saw the creation of the religion of Islam and the rise of the Arabs. Around 635 CE, an Islamic/Arabic army marched into Syria and the Levant, capturing Jerusalem from Byzantium two years later. It was only after the crushing of Byzantine rule by Muslim armies that the Jews were again permitted to return to Jerusalem, Jews and Christians living harmoniously with their Islamic neighbours in the Muslim-dominated city.

In the following centuries, pilgrims from all three religions trekked to the Holy City, until the 11th century when the Seljuk Turks invaded and captured the area. The Turks, who were followers of Islam, banned Christian pilgrimages and placed other restrictions on the Christian religion. Restoring Jerusalem as a Holy Christian city therefore became the objective of the Crusades as proposed by Pope Urban II at the Council of Clermont in 1095. Jerusalem fell in 1099, resulting in many of the Muslim and Jewish inhabitants being killed by the invading Christian army.

Following the capture of Jerusalem administrative control needed to be established. In common with the rest of Europe and the prevailing feudal concepts of the time, a kingship was created with a hierarchy of supporting nobles. It became known as the Kingdom of Jerusalem. As the Christian armies gradually took control of more and more territory, this kingdom ultimately extended to include most of modern Lebanon, the Levant, Syria, and large areas of modern Jordan. It was supported by the two remaining entities of the former Roman Empire: the Holy Roman Empire in the west of Europe with its administrative heads being the Emperor and Pope, and the Byzantine Roman Empire based in Constantinople.

The Knights of the Holy Sepulchre in Jerusalem

This Order is sometimes recorded as being the first of the official military Orders of Knighthood. Godfrey de Bouillon is credited with having led the Christian army in the successful First Crusade. Following that victory Godfrey was awarded the title 'Protector of the Holy Sepulchre'. He died a year later.

Long before this invasion, a group of monks of the Augustine Order are known to have been in Jerusalem and although the city was under Islamic control, care of the Holy Sepulchre was entrusted to them. Godfrey's brother, Baldwin I, on becoming King of Jerusalem defined them as knights. The Augustine habit was white, and according to tradition they were encouraged to embroider on the breast of the habit a symbol which today is known as the Jerusalem Cross.

The crosses were red in colour and the five images (the large cross surrounded by four smaller ones) symbolised the five wounds that Christ is believed to have suffered at the time of the Crucifixion. Amongst the obligations of Augustine Rule was a requirement to fight against the Saracens, protect pilgrims, redeem Christian captives and hear Mass every day.[35]

The Order existed for well over 200 years. When the Christian armies were finally defeated and driven out of the Holy Land in 1291, the Order is believed to have moved to Perugia in Italy and was finally integrated with the Knights Hospitallers in their base on the island of Rhodes. As an independent organisation it therefore declined and almost disappeared. The Augustine monks of the Holy Sepulchre survived, however, and went on to have hundreds of monastic houses throughout Europe.

Several attempts have been made to regenerate the Military Order over the centuries. One such attempt was made by Philip II of Spain in the mid-16th century, but all such attempts ultimately faltered.

Where are the Knights of the Holy Sepulchre now?

This Order is one of two religious Orders that are recognised by the Holy See (the Pope). Constituted as the Equestrian Order of the Holy Sepulchre, it is predominantly an Order of the Roman Catholic Church and is offered to men and women over 25 years of age whom the Church considers have upheld, promoted and encouraged its work and have taken an active community role. Its sole stated purpose relates to religious and charitable matters.[36]

The Sovereign Military Order of St John of Jerusalem

Of all the Orders of Knighthood that have existed, this was arguably the foremost of the spiritual or religious Orders, and the longest surviving. For 700 years, monastic life had in the main followed a pattern of prayer and veneration of the deity that had been set down by the monk St Benedict in the 6th century after he had founded a monastery at Monte Casino. The Order of St John was something new.

Quite how the Order started is unknown, but it is conjectured that it may have descended from Augustinian monks who established a presence in Jerusalem around the middle of the first millennium CE. Notwithstanding such conjecture, many references attribute its prominence to the result of the work undertaken by an Augustinian monk later known simply as the Blessed Gerard, who founded a hospital comprising a hostelry and infirmary next to the church of St John the Baptist near Jerusalem. Hence John the Baptist became closely associated with the Order.

Various references suggest that for several centuries there may have been some form of infirmary on or near the site. With Jerusalem having been invaded several times, a number of previous structures had been destroyed. However, some time prior to the First Crusade it seems that a group of merchants from Naples gained permission from the Caliph of Egypt to build a small house near the Holy Sepulchre.[37] This was probably accommodation for themselves and other friendly merchants visiting the city. They also built a small oratory attached to the house as a place for public speaking, a place that could be used for an early form of preaching. It was a highly regarded skill and to be effective needed preparation and practice. Oration was the skill of rhetoric, which is still regarded as an important element of the liberal arts.

The house built by the merchants was apparently later occupied by a group of monks who provided a small hostelry for pilgrims. The number of pilgrims visiting Jerusalem grew in number, especially after 1099. Sadly, many were robbed and murdered or simply suffered from a range of ailments they had acquired during their journey. So the monks built a large hospital for the accommodation of sick pilgrims. Nobody was turned away, irrespective of their means, their age, nationality or religious conviction.

In the 11th century, public hospitals in Western Europe were rare. Sick individuals were usually cared for by other family members. Most monasteries and nunneries had small infirmaries, mainly to care for their sick brothers and sisters, but some had facilities that enabled travellers, the poor and displaced to seek help. Treatment relied heavily on herbal remedies; surgery was extremely basic and administered without painkillers or anaesthetics. For the most part there was a realisation that a sick person needed rest, warmth, good food and clean water, beyond which recovery was slow, but for most people it was a process of self-healing. Pilgrims who had taken advantage of the available facilities would make a donation to the hospital on their departure.

The hospital and its organisation gained in stature and reputation. From 1099, the monks were required to show loyalty and obedience to the Patriarch of Jerusalem and in 1104 they were confirmed as knights.[38] The order received papal approval through a bull issued by Pope Paschal II in 1113, after which their wealth and influence grew. In 1120, Pope Adrian IV not only confirmed their rule but accepted them under papal protection, a situation that bestowed many privileges and exempted them from paying tithes. Thus the Sovereign Military Order of St John of Jerusalem was created, better known perhaps as the Order of St John or more usually the Knights

Hospitallers. Once it had received papal blessing, the fame of the Order grew as did its wealth as nobles throughout Europe pledged money and land to finance its work.

In its original form the Order operated on two levels: providing hospitals to care for the sick and a military wing whose job was to protect pilgrims. Having achieved acclaim as an institution that cared for the sick, it is a puzzle to many historians why it then took up arms and developed a military capability. However, by about 1140, it seems to have had a large contingent of men in arms, the primary stated reason being for the protection of pilgrims on the roads to Jerusalem. No doubt this protection also extended to the monastic settlements and houses that the Order had established. Their military role, however, quickly changed and they were deployed, along with other knights, in the vanguard of Christian armies that over the next 150 years were locked in battles with opposing Islamic forces.

Despite the early success of the First Crusade, Christian armies were gradually defeated until 1291 when they were finally forced from the Holy Land and the surrounding territories.

In the intervening years, the island of Cyprus had been in Christian hands, so the Knights Hospitallers relocated there. However, they were soon caught up in a range of political manoeuvres. The Grand Master of the Order therefore decided they should have a location of their own. He selected the island of Rhodes and the Order moved there in 1309. They established an imposing presence, many of their buildings surviving to the present day. Having established a new home, they became known as the Knights of Rhodes.

The defeat of the Christian armies in the Holy Land left Roman Byzantium as the last remaining Christian-dominated area of the eastern Mediterranean. It became the focus of ongoing battles with Islamic forces until it too was overrun and defeated in 1480 by the capture of Constantinople. It was not long before the Knights of Rhodes/Hospitallers were again in conflict with Islamic forces. In 1522, an invading Islamic navy laid siege to Rhodes. After several months the knights were forced to surrender and they moved to Sicily.

In the intervening years, the Order of the Knights Templar had been dissolved and their property redistributed to the Hospitallers. With substantial holdings of property throughout Europe there was a need for a proper means of accountable administration. So the Hospitallers' estates were organised into administrative groups based on language and were called 'tongues'. Eight such administrative areas were created and were ruled over by a prior, or a grand prior if a 'tongue' had more than one priory. Thus when the knights were forced from Rhodes, they had a range of other priories to distribute their members amongst. It was not an ideal situation and the Hospitallers sought a new permanent home.

At the time Sicily was a kingdom in its own right, ruled over by the Holy Roman Emperor Charles V (Charles I of Spain). His territorial domain included the Mediterranean islands of Malta and Gozo, which he gave to the Knights in 1530. The military wing became the Knights of Malta yet was still known as the Knights Hospitallers. It was a strategic decision as well as a gesture of goodwill and support. Islamic forces at that time controlled the whole of North Africa, the Levant and the eastern Mediterranean territories that had made up the Byzantine Empire. It was realised that Malta and Sicily were strategic centres for repelling a possible Islamic invasion directly into Italy, thereby threatening the whole of the Holy Roman Empire and the Christian religion. Malta would be the first stepping stone in such an invasion and therefore it had to be held at all costs.

In the eastern Mediterranean the area that had previously been known as Byzantium had been absorbed into the new Ottoman Empire. Having defeated the knights at Rhodes, the Ottomans were now perplexed at finding them again establishing a new fortified home on Malta. In 1565, a large invading force attacked Malta. Records suggest that the Grand Master of the Order, Jean Parisot de la Vallette, had only some 700 knights and 8,000 foot soldiers at his command to defend against an invading force of about 40,000 men.

In the face of such fierce opposition La Vallette retreated to a fort known as St Elmo at the entrance to what is today Valletta harbour. The Ottomans laid siege and constantly fought to overwhelm the inhabitants. Against such overwhelming odds La Vallette and his men held out and inflicted heavy casualties on the invaders to the extent that their attacks became increasingly lacklustre. In the meantime, a small force of reinforcements had arrived on Malta from Sicily. Fearing it to be a large force, the Ottomans retreated.

It is believed that when the siege ended, La Vallette had only 600 men capable of any form of fighting, and many of them had previously been wounded. This event, known as the Great Battle of Malta, is regarded as a great victory for the knights after having endured so many setbacks in the previous 250 years. According to material on the island of Malta, it may have been the last battle that a group of knights fought in their own right and ended a period of 550 years when leading in military activity was almost the sole prerogative of specific Orders of knights.

This Order has thus been known by several names: the Knights Hospitallers, the Knights of St John of Jerusalem, Rhodes and Malta. Today this organisation is also known as the Knights of Malta. In the United Kingdom, it is known as the Most Venerable Order of St John.

The French Revolution and the rise of Napoleon Bonaparte resulted in Protestantism spreading through what had previously been countries almost entirely dominated by the Catholic religion. As Napoleon expanded his republican empire so Malta was invaded by his forces. Instead of resisting this invasion, the island surrendered. This resulted in the resignation of the Grand Master, Count von Hompesch, in June 1798. With the island under French administration the Order was again without its own home and was offered sanctuary in Russia by Csar Paul. By virtue of Count von Hompesch's resignation as Grand Master the Order was without a supreme head. The Csar was therefore elected as Grand Master, a move that did not find favour with the Vatican, so the Pope was assumed to be the holder of the role.

In the reign of Pope Pius IX (Pope from 1846 to 1878) there was a strong movement for the unification of Italy as a single country. This in turn would have meant that several of the so-called Vatican States, a source of considerable income to the Vatican and Catholic Church, would have been lost. It was against this background that a Church Convention was held in Geneva in 1864, to which representatives of the Order were summoned, attending with the same status as any of the nations of Europe that were also present. Pope Pius IX died in 1878. The following year his successor, Pope Leo XIII, reinstated the role of Grand Master by appointing an Austrian, Geschi di Sancta Croce, to the position. Since then, the Order has returned to Malta, but its permanent headquarters remain in Rome.

With the appointment of the new Grand Master in 1879, the Order was no longer considered a military Order but instead concentrated its efforts in the field of medicine, hospital care and the provision of ambulance services during periods of war or natural disaster. In this respect it has returned to its original role. The Order is also accredited with Observer status at the United Nations.

To be admitted to the Order one must meet the following qualifications: descent from nobility for four generations, committed to the Catholic faith, have reached the full legal age (nominally 21 years), possess integrity of character, and a corresponding social position.[39]

The Most Venerable Order of St John of Jerusalem

When Henry VIII was on the throne of England he sought a divorce from his queen, Catherine of Aragon. When the Pope refused to sanction the divorce Henry closed the abbeys and monasteries, created the Church of England and effectively distanced himself and the country from the Holy Roman Empire. It was the endorsement of Protestantism in Britain.

The closure of the abbeys and monasteries resulted in the retreat from Britain of nearly all the houses of the various monastic orders then prevailing. Property held by the Hospitallers was returned to the Crown and reassigned for use by others. Thus the Sovereign Order of St John of Jerusalem no longer had a tolerable presence in Britain.

This situation continued until the early decades of the 19th century when a group of committed individuals attempted to form an English Order of St John. However, little progress was made. Rome did not recognise their efforts and no major charitable activities seem to have been embraced. With a strong desire to see a revival of the Order, three prominent men of their times – the Duke of Manchester, Sir Edmund Lechmere and Sir John Furley – were able to acquire the freehold of the gatehouse of a former priory of the Order of St John/Knights Hospitallers at Clerkenwell, London, in 1874, and thereby establish a permanent base in what had been the main centre of the Order during the medieval period.

The mid-1800s was a period when the industrial revolution was at its height. What Sir John Furley realised was that there was a need to provide rapid and caring assistance to an increasing number of accident victims whether as a result of railway collisions or in mines, steelworks, potteries and mills. Just as there were industrial accident victims, so too there were battlefield casualties in times of war. Florence Nightingale had demonstrated in the Crimea that care, attention to hygiene, and the proper marshalling of medical equipment and supplies saved lives. The first ambulance service had been established in the Potteries district of Staffordshire in 1873. Furley recognised that by training volunteers in first aid, not only could accident victims be attended to quickly but an experienced group of individuals would be made available for battlefield assistance in the event of hostilities. This was entirely in keeping with the original ideals that had motivated the Hospitallers in Jerusalem some eight centuries earlier. Bringing all these skills and knowledge together resulted in the formation of the St John Ambulance Association in 1877. In May 1888, Queen Victoria granted the organisation a royal charter. Today the Most Venerable Order of the Hospital of St John of Jerusalem in recognised as a chivalric Order of the Crown with an influence that extends across the globe and embraces current and former Commonwealth countries.

The Order of the Poor Soldiers of Christ
and the Temple of Solomon

The members of the Order were amongst the first of the Orders of military knights acknowledged by the Pope at the time of Crusades in the 12th century. They were political ambassadors and effectively founded the first pan-European bank, introducing the first bank cheque and the concept of letters of credit. They provided finance to the kings of Europe. They were innovative architects and builders. They were traders. They were farmers. They were monks. They were warriors. But, first and foremost, they were committed to their religion. They are more usually known simply as the Knights Templar.

Over the past 200 years so much has been written about the Templars, yet this book would not be complete without them for they were arguably the second of the military Orders of Knighthood founded and acknowledged by the Church. Their influence greatly outstripped their founding principle and the reputations of almost all other Orders.

They have been a source of interest and speculation to many writers, not least perhaps because of their meteoric rise to prominence in the 11th and 12th centuries, and the speed, ruthlessness and vicious manner of their downfall. Some believe they were the basis on which Freemasonry was founded. Some believe they discovered North America long before Christopher Columbus. Some believe much of their great wealth is secretly buried in America or Nova Scotia (New Scotland). Some believe that Switzerland was founded on the ideals of the Templars, and that its banking industry owes much to the original systems developed by these knights. Some believe that a church in Scotland, supposedly built by their descendants, is the hiding place for the long lost Ark of the Covenant.

Then, in 2001, a document was discovered in the archives of the Vatican. It vindicates the Templars against the charges levelled at them at the time of their downfall. Yet behind their outward persona there lurks a Great Secret.

Notwithstanding any of the speculation that surrounds the Knights Templars, one thing is clear. They presented themselves as fearless and formidable mounted warriors during the Crusades. They were usually amongst the first to be launched into battle, charging directly into the opposing forces, and would fight to the last man. In keeping with the concept of the feudal regime of the time, and the structure of armies, it was only the mounted warriors who were knights. They could be drawn only from the noble families of Europe, and had to supply three or four heavy cavalry horses, their armour, weapons and the entourage that supported them.

Most of the details concerning their organisation and battlefield honours are well recorded in historical documents and can be regarded as fact. Much of the information published about the Knights Templar is based on research undertaken prior to the mid-20th century. Since then an army of academics, graduates and undergraduates with access to documents and material have been prepared to challenge stereotypical views based on earlier revelations and interpretations of that material. Sophisticated technology and electronic communications have permitted access to vast libraries of data and promoted discussion amongst acclaimed academics across the world, leading to new information emerging about the Templars. Some is included here.

Let's start at the beginning.

After a call by Pope Urban II for a Crusade to free the Holy Land, Jerusalem was captured by a Christian army in 1099, led by Godfroi de Bouillon.[40] Godfroi was then made Defender of the Holy Sepulchre, but died the following year. His younger brother was crowned King Baudouin (Baldwin) I of Jerusalem, in 1100. It is against this background of a papal call to arms that the Order of the Knights Templar was formed. Much of the historical information developed over the past 200 years and used as a source of reference by many academics and writers has created a conventional and previously accepted view of events. However, the information now coming to light has caused some of the conventional opinions to be challenged. For clarity, in this section these differences are discussed under the headings 'Conventional view' and 'Revised information'.

Conventional View

Although the circumstances and timing of their venture are a trifle obscure, most reference books state that a group of nine men set out from northern France for Jerusalem, led by Hugues de Payen, a nobleman from the Champagne district. They arrived in Jerusalem in 1118 and presented themselves to Baudouin I (Baldwin), King of Jerusalem. According to genealogists Baldwin I died in March 1118, and his successor, Baldwin II, was crowned in April the same year. It would therefore seem that they arrived in Jerusalem in the first quarter of 1118.

On arrival in Jerusalem, they declared that they would protect the roads used by the pilgrims in the expectation of providing them with security. On all the roads leading to Jerusalem, especially those that led from the Mediterranean coast, pilgrims were prey to bandits who would not only rob but murder their victims. These nine Frenchmen who suddenly arrived in Jerusalem were, it seems, permitted to make part of the original site of Solomon's Temple as their base and stayed there for some nine years. During that time, tradition has it that they did not increase in number but remained the original group of nine. This has raised many questions as to how just nine men could have hoped to protect all the pilgrims using the various roads. Indeed, there is little evidence that they ever undertook such a task.[41] Having obtained quarters above what was believed to have been the site of the biblical Solomon's Temple, they called themselves the Poor Soldiers of Christ and the Temple of Solomon.

Whilst the original founding group of nine knights were camped on the Temple site it is believed that they started digging beneath it and later discovered something of great value. Over the years what they are alleged to have discovered has been the subject of much speculation, including the possibility that it was the Ark of the Covenant, or important documents that might have provided a genealogical connection between some of the aristocratic families that existed in Europe in the early 12th century and those that existed in the Holy Land around 1000 BCE. This speculation implies that a group of men from aristocratic families had been entrusted with knowledge of some dynastic secret and, perceiving that the time was right as a consequence of the First Crusade, had been sent, or chose to go, to Jerusalem to recover materials deemed to have been important to those families. Notwithstanding such speculation it seems that after nine years of being in Jerusalem, Hugues de Payen returned to France on his own and sought help from an abbot who was to pass into history as St Bernard of Clairvaux. Bernard then championed their cause, wrote their Rules of Conduct and presented it to the Council of Troyes in 1128, resulting in the formal acknowledgement of their existence. They thereafter became known as the Order of the Poor Soldiers of Christ and the Temple of Solomon, operating under papal protection.

St Bernard

The following is a summary of the information known about St Bernard, noting that he is a pivotal figure in the story of the Knights Templar.

In the Middle Ages there were two particular monastic orders: the Benedictines and the Cistercians. The Benedictine Order is the older of the two and is named after St Benedict of Nursia (today the town of Norcia in Perugia, Italy). In 529 CE, he founded a monastery at Monte Casino in Italy. Whilst there, he wrote a book in which he set out a code of conduct for monastic life – *The Rule of Benedict*.[42] Like all institutions that have existed for many years, by the 11th century, some 500 years after the founding of the monastery at Monte Casino, innovations had crept into the conduct of Benedictine monastic life that were somewhat removed from the ideals set out originally by Benedict. Thus in the closing years of the 11th century, a small group of monks who believed in a return to the original code broke away from their Benedictine Abbey and established a new monastery at Citeaux, near Dijon in France, in 1098. It was the start of the Cistercian Order. Their uniform was a white robe. Hence this new Order was not the only one with which Bernard is famously connected, but was formed during the First Crusade, and their white robes were later imitated by the Knights Templar.

Bernard is recorded as having been born in 1090, so would have been eight years old when the Cistercian movement was founded. He was born into a family regarded as high nobles of Burgundy. In his early years he demonstrated that he was an able pupil with a love of literature. His mother died in his 20th year after which he contemplated monastic life. In 1113 at the age of 23, Bernard, along with several other young men from noble families, joined the abbey in Citeaux near Dijon, the first abbey of the Cistercian Order to be founded. We are given to understand that Hugues de Payen then prevailed on his cousin Count Hugues of Champagne to make land available for Bernard to establish a new monastery. Within three years of joining the abbey at Citeaux, Bernard and 12 other monks went to establish this new Cistercian outpost in 1115. Bernard called it *Clair Vallée* – Clairvaux.

Establishing the new abbey was obviously hard work and carried enormous responsibilities with it, including maintaining the ideals of the Rule of Benedict that the Cistercians had adopted. Even for a young man of 25 years of age, this work seems to have taken a heavy toll.

Revised Information

On the Mediterranean coast of France, the French Riviera, and a little to the east of the principality of Monaco, is the border with Italy. It is a mountainous area, with steep hills that drop down to the sea. A short distance into Italy, high in the hills, is a small town – the Principality of Seborga. In its documented history we have a further insight into the formation of the Knights Templar.

By the mid-10th century, 150 years after Charlemagne, Europe still contained a number of individual states not ruled over by the Emperor and therefore not encompassed by the Holy Roman Empire. In 954 CE, the feudal lord Count Guido, Count of Ventimiglia, gave an area of land to a group of Benedictine monks. They built a fortified monastery, the foundation of Seborga. It grew to become a commune rather like the Hospitallers, and in the era of the Crusades it started providing care for pilgrims in Jerusalem.

It became known as the Sovereign Order of Castrum Sepulcri. In the same year that Bernard founded the abbey at Clairvaux, 1115, and 160 years after the foundation of its monastery, Seborga became a Principality of the Holy Roman Empire.

In the tourist information of Seborga it notes that Bernard arrived there two years later, in February 1117, and was in poor health. This was the year prior to the recorded arrival of the nine French noblemen in Jerusalem. The information states:

> *'Saint Bernard of Clairvaux ... arrived in Seborga in February 1117, to join Gondemar and Rossal whom he had sent in June 1113, in order to protect the 'Great Secret'.'*

Whatever the Great Secret was, clearly Bernard knew it in the same year that he first joined the Cistercian Order. The information goes on to state:

> *'The reigning prince at the time was Prince Abbot Edward... In September 1118 he ordained the first Knights Templar who formed the famous 'Poor Militia of Christ'. They were Abbot Gondemar and Rossal, Andre de Montbar, Count Hugues I de Champagne, Hugues de Payns, Payen de Mont Didier, Geoffroy de Saint-Omer, Archambaud de Saint Amand and Geoffroy Bisol.'*

From this we have names for the nine French noblemen. It is interesting to note that amongst the party that formed the 'Poor Militia of Christ' are two abbots who were clearly aware of the Great Secret and had been sent there by Bernard five years earlier in the year he joined the Cistercians to protect that secret. In the outline about Bernard, we noted that he joined Citeaux with several other men from noble families. Whether or not Gondemar and Rossal were among them or if they were sent to Seborga as an advance party is unclear. What certainly seems to emerge is that there was a grand plan of some kind and that it probably involved several noble families conspiring together. There is evidence for this. A bishop known as Ivo of Chartres died in December 1115. Prior to his death he sent a letter to Count Hugues de Champagne stating:

'We have heard that ... before leaving for Jerusalem you made a vow to join 'la malice du Christ' that you wish to enrol in this evangelical soldiery.'[43]

This implies that the 'Poor Militia of Christ' was in existence prior to 1115 and was the precursor to the formation of the Knights Templar, for we find in their title almost the same expression 'The Poor Soldiers of Christ...' A group of soldiers is a military force, and the word 'militia' means exactly the same thing. It further implies that the additional element of '...and the Temple of Solomon' was added after they had first visited Jerusalem.

The Seborga information then goes on to state:

'All left Seborga in November 1118, eight arrived in Jerusalem in the morning of May 14th 1119, Hugues de Champagne joined them six years later on the same day at the same time.'

Assuming the Seborga data is accurate, the men arrived in Jerusalem in the reign of Baldwin II, a full year after the usual date quoted in conventional references. Baldwin II was originally from Bourcq, a son of Count Hugues de Rethel. Rethel and Bourcq are both in the Champagne region of the Ardennes, the same area from which Hugues de Payen also originated. Count Hugues de Rethel died in 1118 and the title passed to his son Gervais, which implies that Baldwin II, although from a noble family, was not the eldest son of the Count. Nevertheless this indicates that there was a connection with yet another noble family.

Returning to the Seborga information, it states:

'In 1127 the nine Templars from Jerusalem [returned] to Seborga on the first Advent Sunday of 1127... St Bernard was waiting for them together with Friar Gerard de Martigues... In Seborga in the *presence of all the population of 23 knights and over 100 militias Saint Bernard ordained Hugues de Payns to be the first Grand Master of St Bernard Knights... The consecration with the sword was made by Prince Abbot Edward... In the same day a vow of silence was made between them Saint Bernard of the Knights and the Great Bishop of the Cathars to safeguard 'The Great Secret'.'*

From this, we note that Bernard was an integral and key innovator of the Knights Templar organisation, referenced here as St Bernard Knights.

Return to the Conventional View

In 1128, Bernard then drew up the Rules and Orders for the Poor Soldiers of Christ and the Temple of Solomon. It was presented at the Council of Troyes, convened by Pope Honorius II in 1129, where the Order was officially recognised and confirmed. From then on, the Order operated under papal protection. It paid no taxes or levies, was exempt from tithes, and reported to no one except the Pope. It was a radical departure from the usual organisation of a monastic order, giving them unprecedented power and influence.

There is some evidence produced by genealogists that suggests Hugues de Payen and Bernard were cousins. As mentioned in an earlier section, Hugues de Payen is known to have been a cousin of the Count Hugues of Champagne and was closely associated with the nobility of that period. According to genealogical records, it would seem that Hugues de Payen was descended from Charlemagne through Emperor Louis I the Pious, and Charles II the Bald, King of the West Franks.

Abbot Bernard was obviously well connected and, as we have seen, after lobbying their case Hugues de Payen and the other original knights received formal papal support and protection at the Council of Troyes in 1129. Their rule, or uniform, was a white tabard with a red cross emblazoned on it. Hugues de Payen's strong connections with the ruling nobility of the day – credentials gained as a descendant of Charlemagne – as well as influential ecclesiastic connections through Abbot Bernard, must have all worked in his favour for him to be chosen as the first Grand Master of the Knights Templar.

Thereafter, the rise in the power and influence exerted by the Templars was meteoric. More and more men from noble families joined the Templar cause and provided grants of land as the basis of the security of the Order. Commenting on the support that Hugues de Payen received through St. Bernard, one writer notes that on the return to Jerusalem:

'They [the original knights] had gone west with nothing and came back with a Papal Rule, money, precious objects, landed wealth and no less than 300 recruited noblemen...'[44]

All this was happening some 30-50 years after the invasion and conquest of England by William I, and Norman influence was still much in evidence. Thus it was that, according to some researchers, Hugues de Payen married a Scottish woman of Norman descent, Catherine de St Clair, and established the first Templar Preceptory outside of Jerusalem on the St Clair family lands in Scotland.

The Knights Templar went on to become extremely wealthy, with vast holdings of land across Europe, producing food and breeding horses. They were so wealthy that they loaned money to kings and established what some have referred to as the first European bank. This enabled a traveller/pilgrim to deposit money in, say, London and receive a payment against that deposit at his destination, say, Paris. It was an early example of a letter of credit.

Although the Templars participated in crusading activity, the indications are that their wealth increased to such an extent that they became progressively distanced from papal governance, becoming very much a law unto themselves. Nevertheless, for 200 years they prospered. They built castles, churches, cathedrals, bridges and massive barns for the storage of harvest produce.

By the late 13th century, some 200 years after the success of the First Crusade, the battles for control of the Holy Land were no longer settled in favour of the Christian armies. In 1291, with the exception of a few small fortified outposts, organisations like the Knights Templar were forced from the Holy Land. In the case of the Templars and Hospitallers, they retreated to Cyprus. Whereas the Islamic armies marched under the banner of a single leader, the organisation of the Christian forces was less focused, individuals holding their allegiance to their own Orders. The Templars, who had been established specifically as a fighting force, were blamed for the losses in the Holy Land on the grounds that their diverse interests, wealth and general prosperity had resulted in them losing the fighting edge. So, from about 1274, there had been a suggestion that the main Orders should be merged into a single force. This did not suit the Grand Master of the Temple. There would inevitably be the question as to who would be the overall Grand Master. James Burg de Molay, more often referred to as Jacques de Molay, was the Grand Master of the Temple and agreed to a meeting with papal officials in Poitiers, France, to discuss the issue, and so left Cyprus in 1307. He would never return.

During the early 14th century, the French king Philip the Fair, also known as Philip le Bel, had waged some disastrous wars and was virtually bankrupt. The Templars, who had vast holdings of land in France, used La Rochelle as a port for their ships and also had a substantial treasury based in Paris. Philip was well aware of the great wealth the Templars had within his own realm and apparently decided to acquire it to ease his financial problems. In an effort to secure the Templar treasures Philip is alleged to have murdered two popes and threatened a third, Clement V. Jacques de Molay was godfather to one of Philip's sons. Lured to Paris by Philip le Bel, De Molay was arrested along with a large contingent of the Knights Templar then in France, through a raid that had been secretly organised by Philip and instigated on Friday 13 October 1307. The charges brought against the Templars included heresy, sodomy, denial of Christ and spitting on the cross. In respect to the action taken by Philip le Bel and Pope Clement V, the author of a book published in 1840 states:

'There was a convocation at Vienne in Dauphiny, where the extermination was decided upon in 1307.'[45]

It was this action which has ever since rendered any Friday the 13th as being a day of ill omen.

Despite the efforts by Philip le Bel to arrest the Templars, many of those then in France escaped. Tradition has it that they made their way to Scotland, Portugal and Sweden amongst a number of destinations. Most of the Templar wealth supposedly eluded Philip – on arrival at the Templar Treasury in Paris he apparently found it empty. His scheming had proven to be of no avail. Many writers believe that the bulk of the Templar treasury was transferred to Scotland, where Hugues de Payen had established a preceptory 200 years earlier. However, there is no positive evidence to substantiate that claim. Templar property was requisitioned by other European monarchs as a result of a papal edict issued in 1312. Most such property was passed to the care of the Knights Hospitallers. Undoubtedly, some of the monarchs kept property for themselves.

In England, Edward II had been king for only a few months when the Templars were arrested in France, his father, Edward I, having died in July 1307. Templar holdings in England were not particularly extensive, but they represented a considerable additional wealth. From their earliest days, the Templars had provided great service to a succession of English kings. So when the young Edward was approached by Philip le Bel outlining the reasons for the arrests and actions taken in France and with a request that he arrest the Templars in England and seize their property, Edward was not quick to assent.

At the same time, the loss of Jacques de Molay as leader in day-to-day matters relating to the management of the Order resulted in those Templars in England, most of whom were elderly, becoming disowned, very poor and hungry. Remembering that they were constituted as warrior-monks, the Bishop of York took in those of a destitute state and distributed them around the abbeys under his control. It was not until January the following year that Edward acted, and then only after receiving a papal bull authorising the arrest of the Templars. Even so, many remained in their own manors and houses, living as best they could until they were finally arrested in 1309 and brought before an inquiry and inquisition instigated by the Pope. The inquiries failed to prove any of the allegations that had been brought against the Order, so the inquisitors approached the king and requested permission to torture some of the men being held in the hope that this would reveal the confessions they sought.

Contrary to common belief, torture was not a regular feature of custodial life in England at that time. It was reserved for the most severe cases, perhaps involving accusations of treason or other acts against the Crown. The Vatican, however, ever on the lookout for heretics, had developed exceptional skills and abilities in delivering pain and agony. Edward grudgingly granted permission, but yet again nothing damning against the Templars was revealed. The inquisitors believed that the torture measures used in England were not severe enough and became frustrated that they were not getting the confessions they wanted. They suggested that pressure could be increased if they transferred the prisoners to Ponthieu just across the English Channel, which although part of the English Crown territories of the time was not governed by English law. They could therefore use more draconian torture methods of the type that had been used in France to obtain confessions. Indeed, Pope Clement V agreed with this idea. In his masterly book *The Trial of the Templars* Professor Malcolm Barber notes the following:

> '...a letter from Clement V to Edward II on 23 December 1310 suggests that torture was still not being systematically applied, for the pope offered the king remission of sins and the eternal mercy of God if the trial could be transferred to Ponthieu.'[46]

So much for Christian mercy!

[Author's note: Ponthieu was an area of northern France that had been part of the territory of William, Duke of Normandy. After the

conquest of England by William, the territory was passed down as part of the English Crown lands. It remained as such until around 1435 when it was won by the French king in the Hundred Years War. The Battle of Crécy was also fought in Ponthieu. The capital of the area then and now is the town of Abbeville at the mouth of the River Somme.]

In the years following the arrests in 1307 many accusations were made against the Knights Templar by the Church hierarchy, with charges including heresy, blasphemy and sodomy. The charges levelled at the Templars at the time of their arrest and brought by papal authority at the insistence of Philip the Fair are now widely understood to have been false. A number of Knights Templar were tortured by Philip, including the Grand Master, Jacques de Molay. The power and influence of the Order had, nevertheless, been broken and it was finally dissolved by papal authority in 1314. Jacques de Molay was condemned to death by being roasted alive, not far from the Cathedral of Notre Dame in Paris. James Halliwell uses stronger language:

'... *the assassination of the Grand Master, Jacques de Molay, his murderers being Philip le Bel, Pope Clement V and Squin de Florion.*'

With the Order officially dissolved, the Templars in Portugal disappeared. However, when Clement V died and was succeeded by Pope John, they reappeared and were held in high regard, receiving pensions from their estates. Denis, King of Portugal, was incensed by the actions of Philip and Clement V. When the edict of 1312 concerning the transfer of the Templar property to the Knights Hospitallers was issued, Denis took possession of as much as he could for himself with the intention of restoring the Order of the Knights Templar and returning their property to them.

The King of Portugal sent ambassadors to Pope John who entered into negotiations with a view to restoring the Order.

The negotiations lasted six years and at the end of that period everything that Denis's ambassadors had set out to achieve had been granted, except the restoration of the name, the Poor Soldiers of Christ and the Temple of Solomon. Instead they became known as the Chevaliers (Knights) of Christ, a title not so different from that which they had started with, the Poor Militia of Christ. Despite this effort on their behalf, the new Order failed to regain its former glory.[47] Instead, it found a very different glory, leadership and direction. Amongst those that became Grand Master was Henry the Navigator, and during his leadership the island of Madeira was discovered and claimed for Portugal. Today, the flag of Madeira still displays the emblem of the Knights of Christ/Templar – a red cross.

That, then, is a brief history of the Knights Templar. There is, however, one last point of note. The Great Secret seems to have remained as such, and as noted in the 'Revised Information' above, it was accompanied by a vow of silence made between St Bernard and the Grand Bishop of the Cathars. This vow of silence was clearly regularly made after 1127. In the information from the Principality of Seborga it states:

'In 1611 the last vow of silence took place in the presence of father Cesario da San Paolo, who also became Grand Master…'

In 1207, Pope Innocent III issued a proclamation against the Cathars on the grounds of heresy. It led to what has become known as the Albigensian Crusade, which in the year 1208 resulted in the murder of thousands of people in the area of southern France that borders both Spain and the Mediterranean Sea, known as Languedoc. The doctrine of the Cathars grew rapidly throughout Europe during the 11th, 12th and 13th centuries, so much so that it became a threat to Roman Catholicism and Vatican authority. The Cathars were virtually exterminated at the authority of the Vatican. It is believed that the core beliefs of the Cathars may well have been the basis of the Great Secret. If this is the case, then the mass murders by the Church clearly failed, for as we have seen from the Seborga information, a vow of silence was still being undertaken 400 years later in 1611.[48]

Various writers have pointed out that during the period of the Crusades in the eastern Mediterranean the Templars came into contact with certain doctrines and cultures which they embraced but which conflicted with those beliefs espoused by Roman Christianity. This is not the place to dwell on that speculation. Nevertheless, they may well have been brought into contact with the sciences, mathematics and geometry then understood by the Islamic community. This knowledge resulted in the development of what we have come to know as the Gothic style of architecture. As mentioned earlier, the vast holdings of land and property that the Templars owned resulted in them undertaking some substantial building projects. Throughout the territories in which the Templars operated there are still many wonderful examples of buildings, castles and churches remaining as a testament to their prowess as builders.

Churches in the round were a particular feature of Templar architecture, as were octagonal structures. Of the many round churches that are believed to have been build in England, only five now survive. The most famous is in London, just back from the banks of the River Thames in what is today an enclave of the legal establishment. The hub of this area is the Inner Temple. The surrounding district is known as Temple because it was in that area that the Knights Templar had a major preceptory.

Where Are the Knights Templar now?

After centuries that have involved much speculation about the fate of the Knights Templar, in 2001, Dr Barbara Frale discovered a document in the archives of the Vatican in Rome. The document is known as the Chinon Parchment. The following text was put on public display to mark the 700th anniversary of the assault on the Templars in 1307:

'The document contains the absolution Pope Clement V gave to the Grand Master of the Temple, friar Jacques de Molay and to the other heads of the Order, after they had shown to be repented and asked to be forgiven by the Church; after the formal abjuration, which is compelling for all those who were even only suspected of heretical crimes, the leading members of the Templar Order are reinstated in the Catholic Communion and readmitted to receive the sacraments. The document, which belongs to the first phase of the trial against the Templars, when Pope Clement V was still convinced to be able to guarantee the survival of the military-religious order, meets the apostolic need to remove the shame of excommunication from the warrior friars, caused by their previous denial of Jesus Christ when tortured by the French Inquisitor. As several contemporary sources confirm, the pope ascertained that Templars were involved in some serious forms of immorality and he planned a radical reform of the order to subsequently merge it into one body with the other important military-religious order of the Hospitallers. The Act of Chinon, a requirement to carry out the reform, remained however a dead letter. The French Monarchy reacted by initiating a real blackmail mechanism, which would have then obliged Clement V to take a final decision during the Council of Vienna (1312): unable to oppose the will of the King of France, Philip the Fair, who ordered the elimination of the Templars, the Pope heard the opinion of the Council Fathers, and decided to abolish the Order «con norma irreformabile e perpetua» (bull Vox in excelso, 22nd March 1312). Clement V however stated that this suffered decision did not amount to an act of heretic condemnation, which could not be reached on the basis of the various inquiries carried out in the years prior to the Council. As a matter of fact, a regular trial would have been required in order to pass a sentence, including also the statement of the defensive position of the Order. But, according to the pontiff, the scandal aroused by the shameful accusations against the Templars (heresy, idolatry, homosexuality and obscene behaviour) would have dissuaded anyone from wearing the templar habit and on the other hand, a delay on a decision regarding these issues would have

produced the squandering of the great wealth the Christians had offered to the Order, charged with the duty to help fight against the enemies of the Faith in the Holy Land. The attentive consideration of these dangers, together with the pressure of the French, convinced the Pope to abolish the Order of the Knights of the Temple, just like had happened in the past for much more important religious orders and for much less important reasons.[49]

There are several organisations that use the name Templar or Knights Templar in their title today. There is, however, only one that can claim true descent from the original Order of the Poor Soldiers of Christ and the Temple of Solomon. That organisation is derived from the Knights of Christ – based in Portugal – and is today known as the Order of our Lord Jesus Christ. The King of Portugal is officially the Grand Master of the Order.

There are two other organisations based in Britain that have no direct descent from the original Templars. One is an affiliated Masonic movement known as The Knights Templar. This organisation has a predominantly Christian undertone, although those of other faiths may join, and was formed in the 18th century. The Communications Director for the United Grand Lodge of England at the time the contents of the Chinon Parchment were released stated:

'We don't claim any descent. They originated as a means of commemorating the original Templars and of exemplifying certain Masonic principles.'[50]

The other organisation in Britain is the Grand Priory of Knights Templar in England and Wales. This organisation stems from 1804 when it was founded in Paris as the Order of the Temple. In 1960, the Order was established in England. Two other similar organisations merged with that order in 2003 to create the modern Grand Priory of Knights Templar in England and Wales. This priory operates under an international organisation called Knights

Templar International. It is a non-government group that claims a Consultative status with the United Nations and the International Peace Bureau.

Author's Note: Templars' and Hospitallers' Interests

As mentioned before, when the Templars were dissolved in the year 1314, the Pope requested that monarchs transfer properties of the Templars to the Hospitallers. In England, properties such as Temple Manor in Kent, Hampton Court in Middlesex, and the Temple in London are typical examples of the high-profile properties that were then acquired by the Hospitallers. There were many across Europe that were small but still played an important role in Templar life which are not so obvious.

In the village of Sompting in West Sussex is the small church of St Mary the Virgin. Today a major highway speeds traffic past the church and it is almost invisible to the casual observer. Yet this church is one such property transferred from the Templars to the Hospitallers. It was probably built in Saxon times, just after the era of the Emperor Charlemagne. At the time it was close to the sea for reasons of access, but the coast has retreated nearly one and half miles (two kilometres) in the intervening 1000 years. Following the Pope's edict, it remained in Hospitaller hands until the year 1540 when, during the English Reformation, Henry VIII separated England from the Roman Catholic Church and established the Church of England. During this process the Order of St John was dissolved and responsibility for the church fell to several successive families. In 1888, the Knights Hospitallers were again granted a Charter in England by Queen Victoria. In 1963, the patronage of the church passed back to the Hospitallers.

The Saxon tower was built with stone shipped from Caen in Normandy as well as from other sources. The tower is noted as being the earliest example of a 'Rhenish helm' in England. This style is very similar to the tower attributed to Emperor Charlemagne built in the German town of Aachen. There are the remains of a small chapel on the northern face of the church, which have since been incorporated into what is now known as the Hospitaller Room. It remains today a functioning church for the community it serves.

The Order of the Teutonic Knights of St Mary's Hospital in Jerusalem
Jerusalem and the Holy Land had been captured by Christian armies almost 100 years prior to the Order of the Teutonic Knights having been formed. It was also an era when every monk was not only a member of a monastic community but was also expected to take up arms and defend his religion. At the same time the religious ferment of the period resulted in streams of pilgrims trekking to Jerusalem from across Europe. Amongst these were many from the Germanic areas.

The journey of the pilgrims was long and extremely arduous. Most were poor and walked from their homes to Jerusalem, begging for food and water en route. They were exposed to all types of weather, be it sunshine, rain, snow, the freezing temperatures of central Europe, or the hot glaring sun of North Africa. This resulted in many arriving in the Holy Land exhausted, malnourished and suffering severe ailments. Some were so ill that they did not live to return home.

Tradition has it that a group of German monks founded a hospital in Jerusalem around the year 1120, close to a church dedicated to the Blessed Virgin Mary, to care specifically for pilgrims of Germanic origin. It became a hospital operated on much the same lines as had been established by the Hospitallers. Just as the location of a hospital next to a church dedicated to St John the Baptist resulted in the Hospitallers becoming known as the Order of St John, so the Germanic hospital became known as the Marian Knights.[51] However, this group was not officially recognised as an Order of Knighthood at that time.

The hospital was destroyed in 1187 when the Christian armies were defeated and forced from Jerusalem, the crusaders retreating to the coastal town of Acre (which in the 20th century became part of Israel). It was here that a new hospital was built and officially recognised by Duke Frederick of Swabia in the year 1190 and later confirmed by Pope Clement III to become the Order of Teutonic Knights of the Hospital of St Mary the Virgin. They, like the Hospitallers and the Templars, soon developed a military capability and had as their rule a white habit with a blue mantle on which was described a black cross potent.

This cross is said to resemble the traditional Christian cross but with the bar added at the end to symbolise a crutch, which many infirm pilgrims and wounded crusaders would have used – a symbol of hospital care.

The Order received the full support of subsequent Holy Roman Emperors. Membership as a knight was restricted to the German nobility and although smaller in number, they developed into an influential yet totally different Order from that of the Templars and St John. They are nevertheless recorded as having been an impressive and determined force in battle. This is perhaps best emphasised by the following observation:

> *'The most important early Master was the fourth, Herman von Salza (1209-1239), from near Meissen who, through his own efforts as a diplomatist, considerably enhanced the prestige of the Order... Salza received a gold cross from the King of Jerusalem as the mark of his Mastership, following the distinguished conduct of the knights at the siege of Damietta in 1219.'*[52]

With the final defeat of the Christian armies in 1294, the Order first moved to Venice and then to Prussia, where they built a castle as their primary headquarters. That castle is known today as Malbork Castle, in Poland, having originally been known as Marienburg which means Mary's Castle, after the Virgin Mary that featured in their original title. The castle was built on the banks of the River Nogat, which flows into the River Vistula. This provided an ideal opportunity to charge tolls on vessels using the river. From this fortified position the Order effectively held power over all of eastern Prussia. It continued to flourish until the late 15th century when it faced rebellions over the high level of taxes it was imposing. This resulted in the siege of Marienburg which ended in the year 1457 when the knights were forced to relinquish claim to several territories, including Malbork Castle.

In the same period that the Cathars in south-west France were regarded as a threat to the authority of the Roman Church and deemed to be heretics, so too in the east of Europe there was a considerable influence from what the Church described as pagans, mostly believing in the Arian concepts of Christianity. Just as the Templars and Order of St John were used to crush the Cathars, so the Teutonic knights were used to crush the dissidents to the north and east. The Teutonic knights were diligent in the duty they showed to their religion, so a captured pagan could expect harsh treatment. To be discovered as a non-Christian could result in being committed to slavery for life in the service of the Order.

There was also a further threat that developed. At the start of the 13th century, around the time that the Teutonic knights were being formed in the Middle East, another expansionist army was evolving towards China. They have passed into history as the Mongols, led initially by Genghis Khan. They were ruthless in their conquests, destroying towns, murdering men they captured and taking women into bondage. In 1235, they were well into Russia; by the year 1241, they were threatening the whole of Europe by invading Austria. Thereafter, there was a continuous stream of raids and battles. In Eastern European territories these lasted until the end of the century. For the most part, it fell to the Teutonic knights to meet and defeat that threat.

After the loss of its headquarters at Malbork Castle in 1457, the Order moved to several locations until eventually it became an Order of the Austrian Empire under the Habsburgs. In the early 16th century, Martin Luther embarked on his struggle against the Roman Church. The rise of Protestantism caused conflicts in the Order such that by the time of Napoleon Bonaparte admission as a knight required, at the very least, several generations of German or Austrian nobility in their immediate heritage and profession of the Roman Catholic faith.

The Teutonic Order Today

For most of the 19th century and into the first part of the 20th, the main role of the Order had been in providing and staffing schools and hospitals, which in many respects represents a return to their original role. As with the Order of St John, they have provided medical care during periods of war. After the Great War of 1914-18, there was a major reorganisation of states and the political power base of central Europe. As part of this process, the Order was involved in the abolition of the German monarchy and titles of nobility in Austria.

In 1929, the Order was reconstructed by papal sanction. Because of its Catholic associations it returned to being dominated by Austrian influence, Germany being a substantially Protestant domain. In September 1938, the Order was suppressed by the Nazi regime. Descendants of the once noble families of Germany who would have been associated with the old Teutonic Order are known to have been amongst conspirators that sought the assassination of the Nazi leader Adolf Hitler. After World War 2, the Order was reinstated again in 1947 and has since continued its work as hospitallers.

Other Monastic Military Orders of Note

In the religious wars of the 12th and 13th centuries, kings across the Holy Roman Empire did not wish to be seen to failing both the Church and the Emperor in the Crusades. This resulted in almost every king and nobleman of that era becoming involved in one way or another, resulting in the formation of several other military Orders of Knighthood.

Elias Ashmole composed a list of most of them, following the restoration of the monarchy in 1660 with the reign of Charles II. The following is a summary of such Orders together with further comment based on material contained in the Catholic Encyclopedia and other sources.

Knights of the Order of St Lazarus of Jerusalem

This Order specialised in the care of those suffering from leprosy. Although their main centre had been established in Jerusalem, they received considerable support from King Henry II of England and expanded their houses and properties throughout Europe. When Jerusalem fell from Christian domination in the year 1187, they, like the Knights Templar, established a further base at Acre. The knights were particularly active and lived off the income from the hospitals they ran. This infuriated several popes such that following the loss of the Holy Land in the year 1294, the influence of the Knights of St Lazarus declined and in 1490 Pope Innocent VIII merged it with the Knights of St John, then headquartered on the island of Rhodes.

The Order was reconstituted in later years, but with the death of the Grand Master of the Order in 1572, Pope Gregory XIII made it an Order of the Kingdom of Savoy. It was then merged with several other successive Orders until early in the 17th century it became a part of the Knights of the Royal, Military and Hospitaller Order of Our Lady of Mount Carmel and St Lazarus of Jerusalem. This Order was abolished by Napoleon Bonaparte in 1791.

Although there are several organisations in Europe that claim the title of St Lazarus, there is no official link to the original historical Order. The Holy See has emphasised this in statements issued as recently as 1970.

The Knights of Mount-Joy
Pilgrims visiting Jerusalem had their first view of the city from a point on a mountainous road. It was in close proximity to the point where the Knights of Mount-Joy are alleged to have built a fortified barracks. Their primary role was to protect the pilgrims on the roads leading to Jerusalem.

When Jerusalem fell in the year 1187, the original Order became separated. Some of the knights of this Order retreated to Spain where they were deployed in battles against the Moors, whilst the remainder joined other Orders still active in the Holy Land, including the Knights Templar. Their habit was white, emblazoned on which was the symbol of the eight-pointed cross.

The following list of Orders covers some of those that received papal acknowledgement or were instituted by kings at the time of the Crusades. When the Holy Land was finally lost, some of these orders were merged with the Order of St John – the Hospitallers, the Knights Templar, or merely dwindled from existence or merged with new Orders and operated under different titles.

Knights of St John of Acre (Acon)
Knights of St Thomas
Knights of St Blaze
Knights of the Martyrs in Palestine
Knights of St Catherine at Mount Sinai
Knights of St Anthony in Ethiopia
Knights of St George in Greece
Knights of St James of Santiago
Knights of St Saviour in Aragon
Knights d'Avis in Portugal
Knights of St Michael's Wing in Portugal
Knights of St Gereon
Knights of St Julian de Pereyro
Knights of Truxillo in Spain
Knights of Calatrava
Order of the Holy Ghost in Rome

Knights of St George d'Alfama
Knights of Christ in Livonia
Knights of Jesus Christ in Italy
Knights of St Mary de Merced in Aragon
Knights of the Rosary in Toledo
Knights of St Mary the Glorious in Italy
Knights of St James in Portugal
Knights of Our Lady and St George of Monefa
Knights of Christ in Portugal
Knights of the Passion of Jesus Christ

A series of new military Orders were established after the loss of the Holy Land. New wars or battles were fought protecting the boundaries of Europe. For example, the Ottoman Turks continued an insurgency in the eastern Mediterranean, threatening ultimately to engulf Austria. Thus, during the reign of the Emperor Frederick III, an Order known as the Knights of St George in Austria and Carinthia was founded with the objective of securing the borders of Germany, Hungary, Austria, Styria and Carinthia, the last two places being major states of Austria.

Two of the most famous Orders to emerge after the brutal suppression of the Knights Templar in the year 1307 were the Garter and the Golden Fleece.

The Most Noble Order of the Garter
'The Order of the Garter is the most senior and the oldest British Order of Chivalry and was founded by Edward III in 1348,' so notes an official statement on the British Monarchy.[53]

The Order was founded just 40 years after the arrest of the Knights Templar when their exploits would have still been retained in living memory. The passing of the Templars and the failure of the Christian armies to both win and retain the key areas of the Holy Land sacred to Christians left many nobles without the focus of purpose that had dominated the previous two hundred years. To be a knight of the original religious Orders demanded, amongst other criteria, an oath of obedience and loyalty to the Grand Master. In the secular world, kings could equate to being masters. The Order of the Garter was one of the first secular Orders of Chivalry and has become one of the most famous in the world.

The most widely held legend about how the Order of the Garter started is that at a ball in Calais, then a territory of the English Crown, the garter of a lady, Joan, Countess of Salisbury, (or possibly her mother-in-law, Catherine) dropped casually from her leg and onto the floor. King Edward III, seeing this, stooped down and picked it up. Having done so, he looked about the room and noted that a number of the nobles then present were smirking and smiling. Edward admonished them by saying in Old French *Honi soit qui mal y pense*, which can be translated as 'Shame to him who thinks evil of it' or 'Evil be to him who evil thinks'.[54] He added:

> *'that shortly they should see that Garter advanced to so high an honour and renown as to account themselves happy to wear it.'*[55]

However, according to Ashmole in his published work on the Garter in the year 1672, there is no mention of such an event in any official documents of the time, nor for a period of 200 years thereafter. There is also some doubt that a lady by the name of Joan was a Countess of Salisbury at that time. Other legends associate the garter with having been that of the Queen or the King's mistress. If it had belonged to the Queen, however, the fact that her husband picked it up would hardly warrant anyone at court mentioning or recording the incident; furthermore, there is no authentic evidence to suggest that the King had a mistress.

A further, and more believable, legend has it that during the Crusade in the year 1191, King Richard I led a group of English knights on a prolonged siege at Acre in Palestine. His men were weary from the prolonged fight and he was looking for a way to raise their spirits. He found some leather straps which he made into thongs and distributed amongst his knights to wear as a garter with the assurance that if they fought hard and valiantly they would be well rewarded. It is suggested that this gesture provided the origins of the Order of St Thomas of Acre (Acon) previously listed, which is recorded as being unique in having knights only of English descent in its ranks, and was dedicated to St Thomas Becket. Ashmole suggests that the memory of Richard I's actions may well have provided the background for the title of the Order of the Garter.

Honi soit qui mal y pense is an expression that features on badges and insignia of the Order even to this day. It would be a good expression for silencing one's critics. Certainly at that time Edward was in need of rallying his noblemen as he sought to protect his territorial claims in northern France. Despite the fact that the Order of St Thomas seems a serious contender for the origin of the title, it appears that the legend of King Arthur may have a greater claim.

Edward III would have been aware, even at an early age, of the exploits of his grandfather – Edward I, Longshanks – a strong king who had been actively involved in crusading campaigns over a period of four years from 1268 to 1272, the latter date being when he came to the throne.

Edward I was 43 years of age when he became king and was therefore an experienced and battle-hardened campaigner. He had been involved in several campaigns on British soil, even before joining the Crusades. He knew many knights, who he could trust and how to handle diplomatic conflict. The reign of Edward II, his son, was quite the reverse and was not bestowed with glorious memories. He inherited the throne when he was around 23 years of age so was far less experienced than his father. By that time the crusading Christian armies had been forced to leave the Middle East and England was reasonably calm. Thus Edward II could indulge in what he considered to be the good things of life and as a consequence of having not endured the hardships of the knights that had gone before, lacked experience and exposure to the processes of being hardened. He is recorded as having been indecisive. He lacked military planning skills and had been defeated in battles with the Scots and lost territories in France his father had fought to secure.

Edward I died a few months before the raid on the Knights Templar in Paris by Philip le Bel, and Edward II had to deal with the political effects on England almost immediately on becoming king. Being such an ineffectual monarch, after some 20 years on the throne he was given an ultimatum by parliament to stand down in favour of his son. He agreed and was taken into secure custody at Berkeley Castle, Gloucestershire, in the winter of 1327. According to tradition, Edward II was murdered the following autumn by being leapt upon during the night and rolled up in his mattress so as not to be able to move. Then, because he was a homosexual, and to purge him, he was folded double and a copper tube pushed into his rectum into which a red hot poker was inserted. Thus on death no trace of external injury was visible despite the excruciating pain he would have experienced.

Edward III had gained the throne at a very young age after his father's forced abdication, assuming the throne of England when he was just 14 years of age. He reigned for the next 50 years. As with his grandfather, it was a reign frequently punctuated by wars in which he sought to regain the territories his father had lost in France. In the middle of his reign he also had to face the plague – the Black Death – that reduced the population of Europe by around half.

From the notes recorded earlier in this book, the legend of King Arthur was clearly well established by the early 14th century when Edward III came to the throne, having received mention in a work called the *History of the Kings of Britain – Historia Regum Britanniae* written in the early 12th century by Geoffrey of Monmouth. Thus we have the coming together of several strands of influence: the legend of King Arthur and his knights; the courage of the fighting knights of the various Orders of the Crusades, especially the Knights Templar and the surviving Order of St John; the use of a garter as the background to the formation of the Order of St Thomas which was created by a former king of England; and a king in need of securing his position and requiring the sure support of his noblemen. The young Edward clearly needed men around him he could trust and who would support him on his future campaigns; he also needed to build alliances that he could call on, and establish a secure base from which to rule his kingdom. Windsor Castle and the legend of King Arthur seem to have provided the basis for the development of this great mix of expectations.

'…and being engag'd in war for the recovery of his right to France, made use of the best martialists of the age, did thereupon first design (induced by its ancient fame) the restoration of King Arthur's Round Table, to invite hither the gallant spirits from aboard and endear them to himself…upon New Years day A.D. 1344 he issued out Letters of Protection for the safe going and return of foreign knights, to try their valour at the solemn Justs to be held there on Monday following the Feast of St Hilary… And these Letters of safe conduct continued in force until … the 18th year of his reign'.[56]

It is clear from this statement by Ashmole, that Edward III was building his alliances and recruiting fighting knights, testing them out in jousts and building what today we would call an army of mercenaries. He was just over 30 years of age and clearly shrewd. After these festivities in the year 1344, he ordered workmen to erect a particular building at Windsor, wherein he placed a Round Table of 200 feet diameter,

'…to which building he gave the name of The Round Table.'[57]

The tournaments that started in the year 1344 became an annual event, supplemented in the evenings by balls and dancing at which ladies were obviously present. It is therefore conjectured that it was at one of these balls that perhaps the garter of either Joan or Catherine, Countess of Salisbury, slipped to the ground and Edward III, noting the reaction of some of his nobles, and that the event was subsequently and frequently commented on, used that incident to name the Order with the word Garter in its title. The fact is that today nobody is exactly sure how the title came into being. What is clear is that by his thirties, Edward III was involved in a range of military ventures aimed at securing and enlarging his kingdom, and military prowess was obviously highly desirable. So a lady's garter connected with the leather thong instigated by Richard I to urge courage and determination in battle does have a satisfactory connection. As Ashmole further notes:

> '...King Edward advanc'd the Honour of the Garter, as a denomination of the Order, yet was it not to enhance Reputation to, or perpetuate an effeminate occasion, but to adorn Martial Prowess, with Honours, Rewards and Splendour; to increase Vertue and Valour in the Hearts of his Nobility, that so true worth, after long and hazardous exploits, should not be enviously be deprived of that Glory which it hath intrinsically deserved...'

It seems that there was some jealousy and concern at this unusual and innovative concept, so much so that the French king copied it and in particular invited knights from Spain and Germany to enjoy his hospitality, lest those same knights should become too friendly with Edward and undermine the security of his kingdom.

Irrespective of the conjecture and fable that has built up around the formation of the Garter, the official opinion at the start of the 21st century is that it was established to reflect the legend of the King Arthur and the Knights of the Round Table.

> *[Author's note: Historians have long argued that a building to house the Round Table made for Edward III may never have existed, as no obvious evidence of such a structure remained. In August 2006, a television programme that looks at archaeological sites, Channel 4's* Time Team, *undertook an excavation of the area at Windsor Castle where it was believed that the Round Table built by Edward III may have been located. Evidence of such a building was discovered. However, the Round Table may not have been a table set on legs, as we normally imagine, but a large circular stage on which various entertainments were performed. This might have been surrounded by a cloister-style arcade, into which a continuous table was installed,*

or tables set out, such that visitors were offered some protection against the elements, and in which the King and his invited guests would wine, dine and enjoy the festivities.]

The Garter Ensigns

'The Habit and Ensigns of this Most Noble Order are most eminently distinguishable and magnificent, and consist of these particulars... Garter, Mantle, Surcoat, Hood, George and Collar.'

So observed Ashmole in the reign of Charles II. He notes that the Garter, Mantle, Surcoat, and Hood were all defined in the reign of Edward III, but the George and Collar, known as the Great George, were added to the Order in the reign of Henry VIII. The Garter was undoubtedly seen as the most important and respected item.

'It is the first part of the Habit that is presented to Foreign Princes and Absent Knights... and all other elect Knights, are first adorned; and of so great Honour and Grandeur, that by the bare investiture with this Noble Ensign, the Knights are esteem'd Companions of the greatest Military Order in the World.'[58]

Little, it seems, was actually known or recorded about the Garter until Tudor times. It is known to have been buckled to the left leg, just below the knee. Some Garters were extremely ornamentally decorated, depending on the rank of the person being initiated, with gold buckles, pearls, rubies and other precious stones. Charles I apparently went to his execution for treason wearing his Garter on which the motto was embossed using some 412 diamonds.[59]

The Mantle was apparently fashioned along the lines of the toga worn by the Romans. It was originally blue in colour, made from English cloth or velvet, and reached down to the ankles. Over time the original design changed, first to purple, and later embellished with furs.

The Surcoat was an outer cloak. Various encyclopedias describe this garment as having originally been worn by knights over their armour, and as extending down to the feet. With slits at the front and back for manoeuvrability, and held with a clasp around the neck, it was apparently worn to protect the armour from the sun. The sun reflecting from it could provide advance warning of an impending attack, and/or the armour would absorb the heat of the sun, making it extremely tiring and warm to wear, although essential in battle. Today we might call such a mode of dress a cape.

The Hood seems to have become part of the regalia during the reign of Henry VIII. Hoods, like those often seen in images of monks, were a part of dress for the protection of the head from the heat of the sun as well as in inclement weather. By the end of Henry VIII's reign, a distinctive style of hat largely replaced the hood, and so the hat superseded the hood as part of the insignia. In the reign of James I, the style changed yet again to a broad-brimmed hat:

> '... *but in King James's time... hath been usually adorned with Plumes of White Feathers, and Spriggs, and bound about with a Band set thick with Diamonds; so was the Cap for King Charles II.*'

Windsor Castle – The Home of the Order of the Garter

Not only is Windsor Castle the home of the Order, it is also the birthplace of Edward III, founder of the Order.

Windsor has a long history dating from the time of William the Conqueror. Tradition has it that he found the location beside the River Thames ideal for communication, whilst the surrounding woodlands were good for hunting. Thus he built a fortress on the site. Successive kings then added to it over the next 200 years. Edward III enlarged it and reinforced it still further. Chief amongst those responsible for the construction works was William of Wykeham, who later became the Bishop of Winchester and was involved with the development of the cathedral in that city. According to Ashmole, for overseeing the work, Wykeham was paid:

'... One shilling a day while he was at Windsor, two shillings a day when he went elsewhere about the same affair, and three shillings a week for his clerk...[60]

These were substantial sums of money in their time.

The workmen were mainly stonemasons who had to hew the stone, shape it and undertake the construction, plus carpenters. All these skilled workmen were pressed into service by an order issued to sheriffs around the country who in turn had to provide a surety of 100 pounds. The workmen were not permitted to leave the work without the written permission of William of Wykeham. If they did, harsh penalties were applied. Ashmole states that the numbers found and pressed into the work were as follows:

'... London found forty; Essex in conjunction with Hertford, forty; Leicester with Worcester, Cambridge with Huntingdon Forty, Kent, Gloucester, Somerset, with Devon and Northampton, one with another, found also forty a-piece...[61]

Based on these figures, that is nearly 400 masons alone, not to mention the huge force of unskilled labour that would have been required. Their skill was regarded as being so important to the work, in both the integrity of the structure and the speed of delivery that special orders were issued against anyone leaving the building without the proper authority.

'... all persons were forbid to employ or retain them under forfeiture of all they had, and likewise to arrest those that withdrew themselves from the work, and commit them to Newgate...[62]

Newgate was the site of a notorious London prison for centuries prior to the reign of Edward III and remained so until the early years of the 20th century; it was demolished and rebuilt several times in the same location. Today the site is occupied by a pinnacle of justice, the Central Criminal Court, more commonly known as the Old Bailey.

As mentioned earlier, in the middle of Edward III's reign Europe was struck down with the Black Death. This coincided with major building works, and many of the workmen died as a result of the disease. The works on the main body of the castle took some ten years to complete. St George's Chapel came later.

St George's Chapel – Spiritual home of the Order of the Garter
Ashmole states that there was a chapel on the site which had been built in the reign of Henry I and Edward had it pulled down to be replaced by the new chapel. He dates this to around 1361, by which time Edward would have been around 50 years of age.

> '... in the 24th year of his reign, John de Spoulee had the office of Master of the stone-hewers, and had power to provide masons, and other artificers, to whose care they were entrusted.'[63]

Although begun in Edward's reign, it was enlarged by successive monarchs until, in the reign of Henry VII, a vaulted roof was added.

> 'Anno 21 Henry VII. John Hylmer and William Vertue, Free Masons, undertook the Vaulting the Roof of the Choir (a curious piece of architecture) for 700 [£] and finished it by Christmas 1508.'[64]

The vaulted roof was therefore completed about four months prior to Henry VIII inheriting the throne from his father, Henry VII, who died in April 1509. The chapel was completed in 1528 in the reign of Henry VIII.

This roof is a most impressive structure even today. It draws on the vaulting techniques used in the construction of the great cathedrals of Europe, but takes the concept to a whole new level of sophistication. The result is a broad, flat ceiling above a vast open nave that enjoys high levels of natural light from a series of tall, broad windows that surround it. It is a building of such skill, innovation and intricate decorative finish that it is difficult to imagine anyone contemplating the construction of such a structure today, even for royal patronage. One can only be impressed by the effort and organisation that must have been needed to construct this part of the building without the sophisticated scaffolding and materials handling processes that are employed in our modern era.

St George – Patron Saint of the Order

At the time the Order was founded, it should be remembered that the only religion tolerated in Europe was Roman Catholicism. Attached to that religion was a stream of saints and martyrs. A martyr was a person who had perhaps been murdered for pursuing the Christian ideal in the years prior to the faith being universally adopted by the Emperor Constantine. Around 400 CE efforts were made to assemble information about individuals who had been put to death for their Christian religious beliefs. It was a means of remembering them. By about 800 CE, the Roman Catholic Christian faith was firmly founded, and hence an individual would be posthumously elected to sainthood by the Holy See, based more on what they had achieved for the promotion and promulgation of the faith during their lifetime. Thus St Benedict is remembered for setting out the Benedictine Rule and for establishing his monastery at Monte Cassino, which in turn led to the establishment of a number of monasteries founded across Europe throughout the Middle Ages.

St George is described as a military saint and is often depicted on horseback slaying a dragon with his sword or piercing one with his lance. It is this imagery that no doubt led to him being adopted as the patron of the Order of the Garter. Although classed as a saint, he was really a martyr. He is believed to have lived around 250 CE.

Despite the imagery, the reality is that there is scant factual information about him. According to the Catholic Encyclopedia it is believed that he came from a town in Palestine named Lydda, which in earlier times may have been called Lod, founded by Samad of the tribe of Benjamin, as recorded in the Old Testament, 1 Chronicles 8:12. It is further believed that George may have lived and been martyred prior to Constantine adopting the Christian faith as the unifying religion of the Roman Empire. He was clearly a martyr attributed with great powers, because the Catholic Encyclopedia states:

'...*Delehaye rightly points out that the earliest narrative known to us, even though fragments of it may be read in a palimpsest of the fifth century, is full beyond belief of extravagances and of quite incredible marvels. Three times is George put to death—chopped into small pieces, buried deep in the earth and consumed by fire—but each time he is resuscitated by the power of God. Besides this we have dead men brought to life to be baptized, wholesale conversions, including that of "the Empress Alexandra", armies and idols destroyed instantaneously, beams of timber suddenly bursting into leaf, and finally milk flowing instead of blood from the martyr's severed head...*'[65]

There are further legends suggesting that George had come from a family that, in Roman times, was regarded as noble. His parents had died when he was very young and as his father had been known to the Emperor Diocletian, George had sought and obtained a position in the Roman army. He was deemed a good soldier and by his late twenties had been promoted to the rank of a tribune. During the persecution of the Christians by Diocletian, George had declared his Christian beliefs and denounced Diocletian's actions. Being well connected and respected by the Emperor, every effort had been made to persuade George to give sacrifices to the pagan gods, but he declined and was ultimately executed for his beliefs. The image of the dragon is interpreted by some historians as representing Diocletian, with George killing him with a lance to signify the triumph of the Christian religion over pagan beliefs, and on a white charger to symbolise purity.

A tomb dedicated to him was built in Lydda and apparently rebuilt during the Crusades by the Christian knights. Thus all the knightly connecting mythology surrounding Saint George seems to have found its way to England with knights returning from the Crusades in the 12th century, one to two centuries prior to Edward III adopting him as the patron of the Order of the Garter. It is known that just over 100 years after the capture of Jerusalem by the invading Christian armies there was a synod held at Oxford in 1222, at which 23 April was ordered to be a lesser holiday dedicated to St George.[66] Two hundred years later, this date became a major feast day – the feast of St George.

As a consequence of having been adopted as the patron of the Garter, and the Order being the primary Order of chivalry in England, St George has subsequently been associated with the country as a whole. Interestingly, there does not appear to have been any official proclamation of St George being the patron saint of England, despite being often referred to as such by various English institutions.

The Order of the Garter Today

The Order remains today as the most senior and the oldest British Order of Chivalry. For approximately 200 years until just after World War 2, the appointment of knights was based on recommendations made by the British government, but after 1946, it returned to being an honour bestowed by royal favour. The number of knights is limited to 24, plus knights from the royal line. It is awarded primarily to people who have served the country well in public service, such as a Prime Minister, or who have personally served the monarch.

Women were admitted from the early days of the foundation of the Order, but this ceased just prior to the reign of Henry VIII. As greater equality for women in all aspects of British life gathered pace during the 20th century so they were again admitted by a change in the constitution of the Order in 1987. In the subsequent 20 years following that change, the first women to be admitted as Ladies of the Garter are:

1989 Beatrix, Queen of the Netherlands
1990 Lavinia, Duchess of Norfolk
1994 Princess Anne, The Princess Royal and
        daughter of the monarch

1995 Baroness Thatcher, the first woman
      Prime Minister in Britain
2003 Princess Alexandra of Kent, the Honourable Lady Ogilvy
2005 Mary Soames, Winston Churchill's grand-daughter.

The Order still follows many of the traditions which have been forged over the centuries. A person to be raised to the honour of being made a Knight or Lady Garter is invested by the monarch in the Garter Throne Room at Windsor Castle. Having been invested, the assembled knights enjoy lunch with the monarch, followed by a parade and service in St George's Chapel, and the day is completed by a banquet held in St George's Hall, also in Windsor Castle.

The Most Illustrious Order of the Golden Fleece
Whilst the Order of the Garter is the oldest of the post-Crusade secular military Orders of Knighthood, the Order of the Golden Fleece is renowned as having been the wealthiest. The Order was founded in 1430, almost 100 years after the Garter, by Philip the Good, Duke of Burgundy.

Kingdom and House of Burgundy
For over 200 years prior to the anointing of Charlemagne as the first Emperor of the Holy Roman Empire in 800 CE, a kingdom known as Burgundy, with its administrative capital based in Arles, had existed in south-east France, much of which is today known as Provence. This kingdom was formed when the Western Roman Empire collapsed in the mid-5th century. In the mid-6th century, it became part of the Merovingian kingdom and ultimately transferred to the Carolingian kingdom of the Franks under the rule of Charlemagne.

When Charlemagne died in 814 CE his son Louis (Louis the Pious) inherited the Frankish kingdom, but when he died his three sons – Lothar I (Holy Roman Emperor), Louis and Charles – divided the kingdom between them after a period of dissent and civil war. This created the territories of East Francia as a Germanic kingdom, West Francia which covered most of France and the Low Countries, and a central area dividing them that extended from the North Sea to the Mediterranean coast. Lothair inherited the central area which became known as Lotharingia. Historians note that this division of Charlemagne's kingdom of Western Europe into three parts has provided the basis for wars and disputes that dogged Europe from that time until the middle of the 20th century, a period of some 1,200 years.

The old Burgundian kingdom of the Merovingians ceased to exist, being absorbed into the greater kingdom of the Franks. Charlemagne created a new kingdom of Burgundy as an inheritance for his youngest son. With the creation of the kingdom of Lotharingia, Burgundy was attached to it. Over the next 200 years its position changed, and it was further divided until it became a territory of the French Crown, its capital based at Dijon. In the year 1043, the King of France, Robert I, gave it to his youngest son, but when the line of male descendants ceased in 1361 it was returned to the French Crown. Two years later the then King of France, Jean I, established it as a new dukedom for his son Philip who, as fourth in line, was unlikely to accede to the throne. Three years later Philip I married Marguerite, Countess of Flanders and Artois. At that time the Duchess of Brabant, Lotharingia and Limberg was related to the countess, and on her death these titles also passed to Philip's successors. Philip's grandson Jean went on to add most of the Netherlands to his territorial claims. Jean became involved in several skirmishes to undermine the French king, events that were to ultimately lead to his assassination. Jean's son then inherited the title. By the time of his death in 1467, Philip III – the Good – had amassed an impressive list of titles which included Duke of Burgundy; Count of Artois and Flanders; Count Palatine of Burgundy; Margrave of Namur; Duke of Brabant, Limburg and Lothier [Lotharingia]; Count of Hainault, Holland and Zeeland; Duke of Luxemburg; Count of Charolais; Lord of Friesland; and Marques of the Holy Roman Empire. He was also the premier peer of France.

Founding of the Order

Philip the Good was married three times, but it is the third marriage which is significant for the Golden Fleece because it was founded to celebrate his marriage to Isabella, daughter of the King of Portugal, which took place in Bruges on 7 January 1430. Three days later the *Ordre de la Toison d'Or* (Most Illustrious Order of the Golden Fleece) was consecrated.

Europe had been plunged into a range of wars in which various kings sought to strengthen and expand their territorial claims amid rivalries between the different noble families. Equipping large armies of knights and other mounted soldiery with elaborate protective armour had become very expensive. Tactically the knights had become less effective as opposing armies learned defensive strategies to overcome them. Pikemen could easily unseat a knight in full armour, whilst developments in the use of the crossbow, a weapon that had existed for 700 years, could result in the armour of a knight being penetrated by a bolt fired from such a bow. Thus interest in chivalry significantly declined in the late 14th century. However, by the early years of the next century interest was again on the rise. Philip the Good is credited with having had an admiration for the knights of the crusading era and wished to emulate them. From previous sections and comments on knights it will be recalled that several prominent individuals and noble families associated with major Orders of Knighthood had originated from within territories that were under Burgundian influence. St Bernard, Hugues de Payen and the Count of Champagne were all from Burgundian areas and instrumental in the creation of the Knights Templar. It is inconceivable that Philip Duke of Burgundy would not have been aware of these connections.

Bruges was one of the most important ports in northern Europe at that time. Having direct access to the North Sea, it provided the opportunity to ship goods to most of the countries on the Baltic Sea, North Sea, Atlantic Ocean and Mediterranean Sea. The Low Countries that formed a major part of his territorial claim were rich farming lands, ideal for the cultivation of sheep and the by-products of wool and fine lace. Thus, through the income from his vast estates and the trade passing through his port, Duke Philip III of Burgundy became one of the wealthiest people in Europe at that time. It is the immense wealth of its founder that has resulted in the Golden Fleece being regarded as the richest of the Orders.

Philip had been a close companion and ally of Henry V, King of England. Philip's port of Bruges traded heavily with ports in England, which provided significant economic benefits. Henry V achieved success over the armies of the King of France, Charles VI, at the Battle of Agincourt in 1415, a battle in which close relatives of Philip were killed. This battlefield success resulted in Henry marrying Catherine of Valois, the daughter of Charles VI, and thus Henry became the heir to the French throne. Philip III was the premier peer of the French realm and found his loyalties tested by both his alliance with Henry and his support for the French king. Indeed, his grandfather, Philip the Bold, had been regent and effective ruler of France for some years because Charles had been only 11 years of age when he inherited the throne. Burgundian factions had also been caught up in a French civil war about the manner in which the economy of the country was best developed and structured.

It was against this background of turbulence in which the House of Burgundy found itself that in 1422, just seven years after the Battle of Agincourt, Philip III was invited to be honoured and elected as a knight of the Garter. Philip requested that the honour be deferred to a later date, clearly to buy time whilst resolving the conflicts that surrounded him. However, his request was interpreted as the honour being declined. This action has resulted in Philip being the only person recorded as having been offered membership of the Order of the Garter and declining it.

As with the Garter, legends and fables surround the founding of other Orders; there are different opinions as to the reason for the founding of the Golden Fleece, and the origin of the name. Some historians have suggested that Philip III was impressed by the manner, organisation and prestige with which the Garter was associated, and with the realisation that the opportunity to become a Knight of the Garter had passed, he set up his own Order in imitation of it.

Just as a touch of innuendo surrounds the founding of the Garter based on one having seemingly fallen from the leg of a countess, so there is a further fable, with a similar basis, surrounding the Golden Fleece. Apparently Philip was visiting his mistress and entered her chamber without warning, only to find her naked and brushing her hair whilst sitting on a stool that was covered by a sheep's fleece. At this sight, Philip decided that the fleece in question was worth a considerable value in gold and therefore named his Order the Golden Fleece.

Other suggestions are that the name is linked with the Greek mythological tale of Jason and the Argonauts. This mythological tale has many interpretations, one of which is that the Golden Fleece represents the legitimacy of kingship, and that Jason went forth to seek the fleece with a view to restoring legitimacy of his own kingship. Thus Philip was using the symbolism of the Golden Fleece to establish and reinforce the legitimacy of his own position as Duke of Burgundy and premier peer of the Kingdom of France.

As with the Garter, the number of knights was limited to 24, but this stricture on numbers resulted in some of the greatest nobles of Europe being excluded. With the passing of time, the number increased to over 50. Unlike the Garter, whose head has been the sovereign of the country since the time it was established, the Golden Fleece was not, at the time of its foundation, headed by the monarch. Neither was it an Order of the state. It was an honour bestowed by the Dukes of Burgundy and was not connected in any way with the French Crown.

Beginning around 1517, there was a move to reform the practices of the Roman Catholic Church from which the Protestant movement began. The Golden Fleece has always been an institution loyal to the Roman Catholic faith. The Order, as with the Garter, was adorned with a patron, St Andrew.

[Author's note: In Ashmole's Garte of 1672 and the revision of 1715, it notes that the Golden Fleece was founded by Philip II. This seems to have been treated as fact by many eminent subsequent writers from past generations. In more recent encyclopedias the founder has been credited as Philip III, the reference used here.]

The Insignia of the Order

There are similarities between the Order of the Garter and the Golden Fleece, especially in the important regalia. The most significant is the collar. The Garter Collar, the Great George, has a symbol of George and the Dragon that is suspended from it as a jewel of the Order. The symbol of a ram, in gold, is likewise suspended from the collar of the Golden Fleece. It seems that after the Reformation this symbol was of concern to the Roman Catholic authorities as not being in keeping with Christian symbolism. This difficulty was soon overcome when the Bishop of Nevers decided that it should be seen as a reference to Gideon's fleece, as mentioned in the Old Testament:

'Then Gideon said to God, "If You will deliver Israel through me, as You have spoken,
Behold, I will put a fleece of wool in the floor; and if the dew be on the fleece only, and it be dry upon all the earth beside, then shall I know that thou wilt save Israel by mine hand, as thou hast said.
And it was so. When he arose early the next morning and squeezed the fleece, he drained the dew from the fleece, a bowl full of water.'[67]
Judges 6:36-38

Thereafter five other images of the fleece were added to the collar, making six in total, to represent the virtues of justice, fidelity, prudence, patience, clemency and conduct.

Whereas the Garter collar is blue and gold, that of the Golden Fleece comprises a red ribbon that interconnects a series of other symbols.

'The great collar is composed of double Fusils, placed Back to Back, Two and Two together in form of the Letter B, representing it both ways to signify Bourgoigne. And these Fusils are interwoven with Flint-stone (in reference to the Arms of the ancient kings of Bourgoigne) seeming to strike Fire and Sparkles of Fire between them... The jewel is commonly worn in a double Chainet... linked together at convenient distance, between which runs a small Red Ribbon, or otherwise it is worn in a Red Ribbon alone.' [68]

[Note: Bourgoigne is the French word for Burgundy.]

According to Ashmole, there are two mottoes associated with the collar:

Pretium non vile laboris, meaning 'Not a bad reward for labour', and *Ante ferit quam flamma micet*, meaning 'The flint is sent before to yield fire.'[69] There is also a motto associated with the letter B that is included in the collar: *Autre n'auray*, meaning 'I will have no other'.[70]

A further similarity with the Garter is in the stalls of St Saviour's Cathedral in Bruges. In the choir, above each stall, is a copy of the coats of arms of various knights of the Order.

St Andrew, Patron of the Order of the Golden Fleece

Andrew, it seems, was a popular name in Jewish culture 2,000 years ago. It is derived from the Greek name *Andreia*. Andrew was the brother of Simon Peter. They were both fishermen and members of the 12 apostles. The Catholic Encyclopedia points out that as one of the 12, he would have partaken in the Last Supper and been present at other notable events that are recorded in the New Testament.

After the Crucifixion he visited many places as a missionary. The Catholic Encyclopedia states:

'It is generally agreed that he [St Andrew] was crucified by order of the Roman Governor, Aegeas or Aegeates, at Patrae in Achaia, and

that he was bound, not nailed, to the cross, in order to prolong his sufferings. The cross on which he suffered is commonly held to have been the decussate cross, now known as St Andrew's, though the evidence for this view seems to be no older than the fourteenth century. His martyrdom took place during the reign of Nero, on 30 November, A.D. 60; and both the Latin and Greek Churches keep 30 November as his feast.'

Achaia is now part of modern Greece.

The choice of St Andrew as the patron of the Order is a clear statement of the connection with the Christian faith from its earliest foundations. The feast day of the Order corresponds with that of the saint, 30 November.

After Philip the Good

Philip's son, Charles the Bold, succeeded to the title of Duke of Burgundy, together with other titles with which the dukedom was also associated. Charles was involved with many disputes, and battles followed. He was jealous of the king, Louis XI, and tried to unseat him, resulting in a long period of dissent between the two, and he dreamed of establishing a new kingdom of Burgundy with himself as king, even persuading the Emperor to crown him. In his early years he was extremely successful on the battlefield, but eventually fortune turned against him. He was defeated by the Swiss army and killed in battle at Nancy in January 1477. His body was recovered and now rests in the Church of our Lady in Bruges.

Charles, like his father, was married three times. The third marriage was to Margaret of York, the sister of Edward IV, King of England. Charles had a daughter, Mary. At the death of her father, Mary inherited all the titles and wealth of Burgundy. She is reported to have been the richest person in Europe and such wealth attracted the attention of many potential suitors. In August 1477, at the age of 19, she married Archduke Maximilian I of Austria and hence became part of the Habsburg dynasty. Maximilian was the son of the Holy Roman Emperor and offered protection to Mary for her estates. Charles's old enemy Louis XI attempted to seize parts of her dominions but Maximilian's armies defeated them. A few years later, in March 1482, Mary met with an accident whilst out riding with her husband. Her horse apparently tripped, Mary fell off and the horse rolled onto her, breaking her back. She died shortly afterwards. Her tomb can be seen in the Church of Our Lady, Bruges, close to that of her father. All her titles, and the control of the Order of the Golden Fleece, then passed to the Habsburg line.

Maximilian and Mary had a son, Philip, who married Juana of Castile and in so doing became Philip I of Castile. The parents of Juana were Ferdinand II of Aragon and Isabella of Castile, whose marriage had created the territory of Spain we know today. By the marriage of Philip to Juana the Habsburgs became rulers of Spain. Philip died prior to his father and therefore did not become Emperor or inherit his father's titles, but he did inherit those from his mother, such as that of the Duke of Burgundy. Philip, who had been born in Bruges, was not only King of Spain but also had control of large territories to the north of France, particularly the Low Countries.

Philip and Juana of Castile had a son, Charles, grandson of Maximilian. He became Charles I of Spain and Charles V (Karl V) Emperor of the Holy Roman Empire. Inheriting his grandfather's titles as well as those of his father, he therefore held all the titles and domains of the Habsburgs of Austria, Burgundy, Castile and Aragon. Just a few years prior to his birth, Ferdinand and Isabella had financed an explorer by the name of Christopher Columbus to sail west in search of China. His discovery of the Americas, however, led to significant conquest of territory, particularly in South America. All of this new territory was now controlled by Charles V, who also became the Holy Roman Emperor through the Habsburg line. Significantly, the Order of the Golden Fleece also fell within his sphere of control and hence became the primary Order based in Burgundy including the Low Countries, the Austro-Hungarian Empire and Spain.

In his later life Charles's health failed and he abdicated. His son, Philip II, took control of Spain, the Netherlands and Italy, whilst his brother took control of Austrian territories and became Emperor Ferdinand I. At his abdication on 25 October 1555, Charles V, in the presence of various knights of the Order of the Golden Fleece, apparently took his collar and jewel of the fleece from around his neck and placed it over the head and shoulders of his son Philip, thereby transferring control of the Order of the Golden Fleece to a Spanish king. There was, however, a further branch of the same Order that continued to operate within the Austrian domains of the Habsburgs.

Whereas the Garter was established in a permanent home, St George's Chapel at Windsor Castle, the Golden Fleece did not have such a base. Even so, Bruges, the place of its foundation, was seen as its spiritual home, and various chapters were held there, along with its treasures.

The Order of the Golden Fleece today

The interconnection between Burgundy, the Habsburgs and the Spanish Crown ultimately led to the Wars of the Spanish Succession which lasted from around 1701 to 1714. Following those wars, Philip V of Spain, who was descended from Charles V, was acknowledged as King of Spain and held sovereignty over the Golden Fleece. The sovereignty of other domains of the Spanish Crown in Europe was divided between the Habsburgs and the Dukes of Savoy. By virtue of the fact that the Habsburgs gained control over the Netherlands, the treasures of the Golden Fleece were moved to Vienna.

After World War 1, when the Axis powers of Austria-Hungary and Germany had been defeated, the Emperor and nobility were deposed and replaced by a republican government. As Bruges was now a Belgian city, the King of the Belgians attempted to claim sovereignty over the Order but this claim was dismissed. Following World War 2, Austria continued to be governed as a republic. Although the treasures of the Golden Fleece remain in Austria, the

Austrian Order has been decreed as an independent Order of the Habsburgs as opposed to an Order of the state of Austria, and is headed by a surviving member of the Habsburg dynasty. As such, the Order continues to exist with an impressive list of Germanic princes and descendants of past nobility included in its membership. It still retains close links with the Roman Catholic Church.

The Spanish Order also exists, with the King of Spain at its head. The list of persons awarded the honour of membership include many of the kings and queens of Europe, and rulers from other parts of the world. Although established with a Roman Catholic devotion, in more recent times the list has included prominent persons of other faiths.

The Roman Eagle

'... It is older than the Golden Fleece and Roman Eagle, more honourable than the Garter or any other Order in existence...'

This is a statement found on examining the ceremonial contents of one of the oldest fraternal organisations in existence – the Freemasons. The Golden Fleece and Garter have been noted, but where does this reference to the Roman Eagle come from? The assertion that Freemasonry is older than the Golden Fleece suggests it is referring to an Order or organisation of standing that was formed or created prior to the year 1430. However, there is no Order simply known as the Roman Eagle.

Reviewing Ashmole's compendium of Orders of Knighthood, there was an Order called the White Eagle created by the King of Poland in the year 1325. This Order seems to have died out not long thereafter, but was reinstated in the year 1705 and has continued to the present day, albeit with minor interruptions due to political and territorial changes. The President of Poland is today the Grand Master of the Order. Its history, however, does not fit with the opening statement above.

There was an Order of the Black Eagle in Prussia, but this was not created until the year 1701 and continued until the year 1918.

This Order is not mentioned in Ashmole's work of the year 1672, but is included in a revised edition of 1715. This Order too can therefore be excluded.

During the existence of the Roman Empire the army carried before it an image of an eagle, symbolising imperial authority exercised through the People and the Senate of Rome. Its use by Rome extends to about 100 BCE. Thus the single eagle used by Rome seems also to be excluded.

A major influence for Freemasonry is geometry, especially the geometric understanding of the stonemasons' guilds that built the great cathedrals and castles of Europe in the Middle Ages. A major architectural revolution occurred during the existence of the Knights Templar, and St Bernard, who was closely associated with them. St Bernard is credited with being further connected to the evolution of the form of architecture that we know today as Gothic. This architectural style has been derived from a series of geometric figures and mathematical constants that were used in the creation of ancient Greek and Roman designs. It is known as sacred geometry. As the opening statement refers to the Golden Fleece, there is an implication that the Roman Eagle was a device in use or created not thousands of years prior to the Fleece but in reasonable historic proximity to it. There is only one such configuration that seems to fit that requirement – the double-headed eagle of the Holy Roman Empire. It was first used as a symbol of that Empire around the year 1250 by the Holy Roman Emperor Frederick II. He was supposed to have taken part in the Sixth Crusade, but turned back when illness swept through his army.

The symbol of the two-headed eagle is very ancient. It has been noted on archaeological relics from Mesopotamia dated from around 2000 BCE. Its use by Rome, however, seems to stem from the period when Constantine the Great relocated the administrative centre of the Empire away from Rome to the new capital Constantinople, and in so doing established the foundations of the Byzantine Empire. There were, at that time, two administrative areas of the Empire, that of the East and the West. The two-headed eagle was apparently adopted to signify those two domains of Roman rule, looking east and west, with the body signifying the heart based in Constantinople. With the collapse of the Western Roman Empire in the 5th century, the symbol ceased to be used in Europe and it came to be associated with the Byzantine Empire until around the year 1200; it finally collapsed in the mid-15th century.

The Holy Roman Empire of the West evolved from around the year 800 CE. It seems that the two-headed eagle therefore came to prominence around the year 1250 to symbolise the continuity of the Roman Empire through the Emperors of the Holy Roman Empire. This eagle remained a symbol of the Holy Roman Empire until it was dissolved by Napoleon Bonaparte in 1806. The Habsburg line, Holy Roman Emperors and the Austrian Empire were all inter-related throughout the Middle Ages, so it was only natural that the two-headed eagle should become associated with Austria and appear as a symbol on its flag. In turn it was adopted by other countries that had been part of the Austrian Empire, and remains on many flags of Eastern Europe to this day.

Some of the other Orders of Knighthood
The following is a list of some of the other Orders of Knighthood in Europe from the period of the Crusades, most of which existed prior to the Restoration of the British monarchy with Charles II in 1660 and recorded by Elias Ashmole:

The Knights of Our Lady of the Star
Founded in France in the year 1022.

The Order of the Lily of Navarre
Founded by the King of Navarre in the year 1048. Navarre was a kingdom in the area now known as the Basque region on the border of Spain with France, and became part of France in the year 1620.

The Order of the Sword of Cyprus
Founded by the King of Jerusalem and Cyprus in the year 1195, during the era of the Crusades.

The Order of the Bear in Switzerland
Founded by the Holy Roman Emperor, Frederick II, in the year 1213 at the Abbey of St Gall. Part of Switzerland had been in Lotharingia when that kingdom was created after the death of Charlemagne. Some of the cantons merged to become a city state within the Holy Roman Empire. Swiss territory continued to consolidate until in 1499 it effectively became free from the rule of the Holy Roman Empire. At that time the Order was dissolved.

The Broom – Flower
Founded in France in the year 1234.

Knights of St James in Holland
Founded in the year 1290 at The Hague.

Knights of Jesus at Rome
Founded by Pope John XXII in France in the year 1320.

The Order of the White Eagle
Founded in Poland in the year 1325.

The Order of Knights de la Band in Castile
Founded in Castile (Spain) in the year 1330.

The Order of de la Calza
Founded in Venice in the year 1400. Disbanded 1590.

The Order of the Seraphim
Such an Order was founded in Sweden in the year 1134, but seems to have declined. A new Order of the Seraphim was founded by King Frederik I of Sweden in 1748 and remains the premier Order of that country.

The Order of the Sword
Founded in Sweden along with Seraphim. It is no longer awarded.

Order of the Most Holy Annunciation
Founded in Savoy (part of north-west Italy) in the year 1362. This Order still exists today. A primary requirement is to be of the Roman Catholic faith, although non-Catholics are permitted as honorary

members. It was the State Order of Italy until Italy became a republic in 1946. It is now a family dynastic Order in much the same way as the Golden Fleece.

The Order of St Michael

Founded in France in 1469 by Louis XI, it imitated the Order of the Golden Fleece which had been founded by his great rival, the Duke of Burgundy. It grew substantially in numbers so that the value of its award was considered to have been diminished. It was officially abolished in the Napoleonic era.

The Order of the Holy Spirit

Founded in France in 1587, it became the premier Order in France. It was abolished in the Napoleonic era.

The Order of the Holy Ghost

Founded by Pope Innocent III in the year 1216 in the Hospital of the Holy Ghost in Rome. It existed for several centuries until, as the medical profession grew, it was superseded by their expertise.

The Order of the Amarantha

Founded in Sweden in 1645 (though some literature suggests it was 1651) by Christina, Queen of Sweden. The name is thought to be based on Greek, meaning 'Never fading'. It was said to have been instituted to honour a particular lady of that name, considered to have been a beauty, who acted with modesty, courage and charity.[71] Princes and kings were admitted as members. Queen Christina ruled against the background of political and religious upheavals of the time in a country where the crown did not pass to a female, however able. A non-Catholic at birth, she eventually took to the Roman Catholic faith, enjoyed good contacts with the Pope and eventually abdicated in the year 1654 rather than marrying for the sake of retaining the Crown, and the Order ceased.[72]

In the late 19th century, Christina's story was researched in America. So impressed was the researcher by her religious conviction, diplomatic prowess and charitable nature that he established a new Order that continues to exist in many parts of the world. It is an affiliated Masonic organisation, which is open to membership by the wives, partners and daughters of men who are masons, and other women who may be recommended. The Order undertakes considerable charitable activities. It is closely allied with another similar Masonic organisation, also started in America, known as the Eastern Star, which has no historic pedigree associated with Orders of chivalry.

Modern Orders of Knighthood

As an increasing number of countries have replaced their monarchy and abolished or minimised the influence of various nobilities in favour of republican government, so many of the chivalric Orders that were associated with such countries have fallen into disuse. The United Kingdom, however, continues the tradition. The following is a brief outline:

Order	Year Constituted	Founding Monarch	Awarded to
Most Noble Order of the Garter	1348	King Edward III	Persons who have undertaken distinguished service on behalf of the country, or personally served the monarch with distinction
The Most Ancient and Most Noble Order of the Thistle	Legend 809 Possibly around 1500 Statute 1827	James II	Persons who have undertaken distinguished service on behalf of Scotland
The Most Honourable Order of the Bath	1725	George I	Awarded for distinguished military and civil service
The Most Distinguished Order of St Michael and St George	1818	Prince Regent (became George IV in 1820)	For diplomatic services
The Distinguished Service Order	1886	Queen Victoria	Military Officers – special recommendations in times of war
The Royal Victorian Order	1896	Queen Victoria	Services to the monarch
The Order of Merit	1902	King Edward VII	Services to the military, science, art, literature, culture
Imperial Service Order	1902	King Edward VII	Distinguished service for over 25 years as a civil servant

Order	Year Constituted	Founding Monarch	Awarded to
The Most Excellent Order of the British Empire	1917	King George V	A general Order, to persons military and civil, in recognition of outstanding commitments and achievements
The Order of the Companions of Honour	1917	King George V	For service to the arts, science, politics, industry, religion

There was formerly one additional Order of Chivalry: the Order of St Patrick. This Order was founded in the year 1783, but was discontinued from 1922.[73]

Countries where the monarchy still exists such as the Netherlands, Sweden, Norway and Spain have their own national Orders. At the time of writing they comprise the following:

Netherlands: Order of the Lion of the Netherlands
Order of Orange – Nassau
Military William Order

The Order of the Lion of the Netherlands is the oldest civil Order of the country and was established in 1815, after the defeat of Napoleonic forces. The Order of Orange – Nassau was founded in 1892. Both Orders are considered civil honours and are awarded by very democratic processes with recommendations from citizenry and civil authorities. The monarch is the Grand Master of both Orders. The Military William Order was also founded in 1815 as an award for military bravery and is an honour bestowed on military and civil personnel. The lower levels of the Order are still noted as knights.

Sweden: The Royal Order of the Seraphim
Royal Order of the Polar Star

Modern Swedish Orders commenced in 1748. The Swedish state notes that there is no conclusive evidence to suggest that the Order of the Seraphim has any connections with any other Order of the same name in the past. The monarch is the Grand Master of Swedish Orders and the members are regarded as knights.

Norway: Royal Norwegian Order of St Olav
                 Royal Norwegian Order of Merit

The Royal Norwegian Order of St Olav was founded in 1847, and the Order of Merit in 1985. In each case the lower levels are referred to as knights.

Denmark: Order of the Elephant
                 Order of Danneborg

With origins that may have links back to the 14th century, the Order of the Elephant was officially founded in the year 1693. It is awarded to Heads of State and members of the Danish royal family. The Order of Danneborg was established in 1671. Today it is an Order of honour awarded to Danish citizens. Both Orders confer the title 'knight'.

Spain: Order of the Golden Fleece

Details of this Order are contained earlier in this section.

Countries that have discarded the system of monarchy in favour of democratic republicanism have recognised that a means of rewarding individuals for service to their nation is a concept that has its merits. They embody the essence of the original concepts of chivalry – obedience, loyalty and bravery being just a few. One of the main European countries to have adopted this is France, where the *Légion d'honneur* fulfils such a role for both military and civilian honours.

Like most Orders of chivalry it has several grades:
Grand Master – the President of France
Grand Cross
Commander
Officer
Knight

Promotion from one grade to the next requires a demonstrable commitment to the ideals of chivalry and a minimum period of time before each step, or promotion, is possible.

Is There a Value to Knighthoods Today?

What is the value of knighthoods in our modern society? Most cultures of the world have some form of hierarchy with a dominant figurehead. In areas that still have close-knit tribes it is the tribal chief; in our Western society it is a monarch or a president. Whichever form of sophistication the social grouping or society comprises, there are still likely to be bodyguards helping to protect the leader, like those who surround royal palaces in Britain, or secret service agents who act as bodyguards for presidents. They are not all called knights, but there are a few, depending on their nationality and their achievements, who are bestowed with that title.

In Europe, awarding such an honour is a means of showing society's favour, recognising good works, honouring loyalty. It provides a vehicle by which a group of people can transcend layers of government at senior levels and take an active role in influencing decisions. It is like a club where, without the right credentials of membership, admission is not permitted; and if you are not permitted, you are excluded from participating in its mysteries. Such honours provide access to people and events that would otherwise be forever distant.

Almost every major country in the world operates some form of inter-related system of chivalric honour. Today such honours usually recognise the efforts and abilities of the individual in their lifetime rather than being hereditary. Whoever receives such an honour has surely deserved the recognition and respect that is attached to it.

This is probably truer today than when honours were awarded solely in consequence of an accident of birth, or for demonstrating prowess in battlefield butchery as was the case in yesteryear.

Above: Temple Manor, Strood, Kent. Once the manor house of a substantial farm and rest house for important travellers and Templars. *Kevin L. Gest*

Below: The keep of Rochester Castle and spire of Rochester Cathedral, both prominent features in the era of the Knights Templar, viewed from close to Temple Manor. *Kevin L. Gest*

Right: The hackamore style
of bridle, pointing out the
pressure points most likely
used prior to the development
of the mouth bit. *Kevin L. Gest*

Right: A clay image of a
warrior from Cyprus around
700 BCE, 2,800 years ago.
There were no stirrups,
the rider has a shield, and
the reins of the horse show
connection to a device at the
nose, rather than a bit in the
mouth. *By kind permission of
the British Museum.*

Above: A mosaic showing a mounted Roman warrior, 2nd century BCE, without stirrups and spear or lance in hand. Again, the control of the horse is at the nose, not the mouth. *By kind permission of the British Museum.*

Left: An elaborate warrior's bronze helmet (armour) of the Corinthian type from around 600 BCE. *By kind permission of the British Museum.*

Left: Elaborately decorated knee and shin armour for a mounted warrior. Probably from Greece around 470 BCE. *By kind permission of the British Museum.*

Below: Styled torso armour. Probably from Greece around 375 BCE. *By kind permission of the British Museum.*

Right: The throne of Emperor Charlemagne at Aachen Cathedral. *Kevin L. Gest*

3 - Chained as a prisoner, he prays to St Leonard for deliverance from his captivity in Jerusalem.

4 - Sir Hugh de Hatton escapes and makes his way back to England where he is discovered by his herdsman, but not recognised.

5 - Sir Hugh is presented to his wife and offers the part of the ring he had retained, by which she acknowledged him;

6 - Restored to his lands, Sir Hugh de Hatton announces his gift of property for the foundation of Wroxall Abbey in the year 1141.

Section 5

Symbolism and the Knights

It is surrounded by a desert that moves at the insistence of the winds. The sands are hemmed in on all sides by stark hills, denuded of vegetation. In parts there are gnarled rocky mountains as old as time itself. The faces of others are smooth, having been sandblasted over the aeons. Sitting at the base of just such a mountain, in a pass between two rows of peaks, stands a small outpost of religious antiquity. The peak that towers above it is Mount Sinai, where, tradition has it, at its pinnacle, Moses received the Ten Commandments.

This small religious outpost is St Catherine's Monastery. Within its grounds is a flowering bush, which, the monks tell us, has grown from the original 'burning bush'.

St Catherine's is regarded as the oldest working Christian monastery. Helen, the mother of Constantine the Great, had encouraged the building of a chapel on the site, the Chapel of the Burning Bush, sometime around 330 CE. It was later turned into a monastic fortress by the Emperor Justinian over a 40 year period commencing in 527 CE. It is every bit a fortress, with outer walls that in places are estimated at 35 metres (115 feet) high. Although access to the monastic interior today is through a gateway in the outer wall, for the first 600 years of its existence the only way in and out, and for the movement of food or other requisites, was over the top of the wall, using a rope and pulley system the evidence of which can still be seen.

What is particularly remarkable is the ceiling of the chapel. Very dark in colour, it is festooned with images of the stars – a depiction of heaven. But there is a shape at the centre of the ceiling that most visitors would not take notice of. It is an octagon. And the octagon, or sacred octagon as it is known when incorporated into religious buildings, appears in many churches and cathedrals, usually at the highest point of the ceiling. The Holy Sepulchre in Jerusalem is also shaped in the form of an octagon.

Tradition has it that once the Emperor Constantine realised the potential of Christianity as a way of reuniting the Roman Empire, his mother, Helena, visited the Holy Land with a view to securing religious relics that might have been directly associated with events in Jerusalem around the time of Christ. Equally according to tradition, she located Calvary, the alleged tomb of Christ and part of the cross on which he was crucified. The part of the cross she allegedly found became venerated as the true cross. It should be borne in mind that Helena's visit occurred some 300 years after the Crucifixion, but there may well have been a tradition handed down through the generations of local people that enabled the place to be identified with relative ease.

On the site at that time had been a temple built by the Romans to venerate their god Venus. In 70 CE, some 40 years after the Crucifixion, there had been a Jewish uprising against Roman rule which the authorities brutally suppressed, destroying large areas of Jerusalem. Many of the Jews living in Jerusalem at that time fled from the city and it was some decades before they returned in any real numbers.[74] Around 130 CE there was yet another, more determined uprising, as a consequence of which the Emperor Hadrian marched an army across Europe, suppressed the revolt and banished the Jews from Jerusalem. Following this, most sites that held religious significance for the Jews, particularly in and around Jerusalem, were completely destroyed or temples to Roman gods built on the site. Thus, when Helena arrived in Jerusalem nearly 200 years later, the Roman temple to Venus was still prominent. In 326 CE, the Emperor Constantine, having received information from his mother, ordered that the temple be pulled down and a basilica built over the site. Records suggest that it was a magnificent building for its time, being of circular design enclosing the entire site and with a domed roof. The site later became the location of the Holy Sepulchre.

This first basilica was burnt down during an attack on Jerusalem by a Persian ruler, Chosroes II, in 614 CE, in what was a general assault on the Roman Byzantine Empire. The Romans, however, soon won Jerusalem back and Chosroes was killed, allegedly by his own son.[75] A further church and other buildings were erected, taking some 200 years for them all to be completed. This basilica was again circular and enclosed the site, and immediately above the tomb was an octagonal structure. They were destroyed by an Islamic army that invaded Jerusalem in 1010 CE. It is recorded that more, smaller churches were built and later incorporated into a circular basilica that was completed by the crusaders around 1168 CE. This stood the test of time until it was partly destroyed by fire in the early 19th century.

According to various writers on the subject of such symbolism in Christian churches, the sacred octagon symbolises eternity. The octagon is a reference to the number eight. In mathematics the symbol for infinity is the number eight turned on its side: ∞. 'Infinity' and 'eternity' have the same basic meaning – a dimension that has no limits or ending.

From the above it will be noted that in the reign of Charlemagne the basilica enclosing the site of the tomb of Christ would have been that which was later destroyed by Islamic forces in 1010 CE. The oldest cathedral in Europe is one built by the Emperor Charlemagne around 800 CE at Aachen in Germany. This is a remarkable structure, not least because of the link it shows with the concepts of ancient wisdom, a wisdom later employed by religious Orders of Knighthood and within religious rituals.

There is one group of people who knew more about this symbolism than almost any other. They were the masons. Theirs was the trade that had built all the great stone edifices of Egypt, Greece and Rome. They were the people who had designed and built such wonderful structures as Charlemagne's cathedral at Aachen.

The Significance of Symbolism
Do not dismiss symbolism. It is not simply an antiquated concept employed by our forebears. It plays an important role in our 21st century lives, just as it did for our ancestors. In the Middle Ages, an elaborate religious symbolism was attached to flowers and fruits such

as the rose, lily, iris and strawberry. Today there is hardly a major company that does not use the power of symbolism as part of its corporate mantra. The difference is that now we often refer to such symbolism as logos. Thus we find that modern corporations and institutions go to considerable and expensive lengths in the design and presentation of their identity. Their corporate logo – a name, word or graphic –is a symbol of the organisation. It can be used to imply high quality; in some cases it might imply high price as well. There might be an impression of global trade with a strong multi-national corporation to support it, or it might imply a local trusted institution. Hence we find the regular use of geometric symbols, star shapes and carefully crafted graphics appearing on cars, clothing, footwear and appliances, to name but a few.

In the western world there is one symbol – the cross – that carries a considerable amount of subliminal meaning. It is a symbol that implies religion and, in particular, Christianity. The crescent and star image is a recognised symbol for another religion, Islam.

A further example of a widely recognised symbol is that of the International Olympic Committee, organisers of the Olympic Games of the modern era. The design symbolises the coming together of the participants from the five main continents of the world. This symbol alone underlines the power of the visual image: it says so much without the need for words. And that is the essence of symbolism.

In the Beginning was the Circle

To understand much of this symbolism we need also to understand that in the era of the civilisations of Egypt, Greece and Rome they did not have the advantage of sophisticated mathematical formulae. There was no algebra, calculus, zero or decimal point. But they had geometry and used it as a means of solving all their structural problems – and they were very good at it. So when they came to build churches, cathedrals and castles, they resorted to those tried and tested geometric patterns. Some of those patterns came to have a symbolic meaning that was transferred into the design of a structure.

Thousands of years ago, long before the advent of writing, there was a need to ensure that the knowledge gained by a civilisation was not lost with the passing of generations. Thus we learn that the custodians of information to be passed from generation to generation were the priests. They were the sages, or wise men. As they understood geometry, they could see examples of similar patterns in nature. Geometry, not unexpectedly, became associated with the designs of divine creation. As a consequence many such patterns found their way into religious symbolism. For example, the very ancient symbol of the pentagram is often represented in windows of Christian churches to symbolise the five wounds suffered by Christ at his Crucifixion caused by nails through his wrists and feet, and thorns in his head.

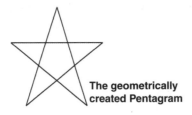

The geometrically created Pentagram

Pentagram proportions in Nature

Three primary geometric forms were used and understood by our ancestors: the circle, the square and the equilateral triangle. The most revered of all the geometric forms was the circle. The square and triangle can both be created from the circle, but a circle cannot easily be constructed from the other two. In particular, it was the centre of the circle that was the most sacred point in geometry. It is from that point that the circle is constructed, and in order for it to be a true circle, every point of the circumference must be an equal distance from the centre. Noting that our ancestors observed numerous geometric patterns in nature, and that the deity was credited with creating the world and all things in it, we can understand why those same ancestors believed that such divine creation must have started with the centre of a circle. The centre of the circle therefore became the sacred place from which all things had originated. Whilst today, with our accumulation of knowledge gained over thousands of generations, we may find such ideas bizarre, to them it was an entirely logical deduction, and, in many societies, still holds sway.

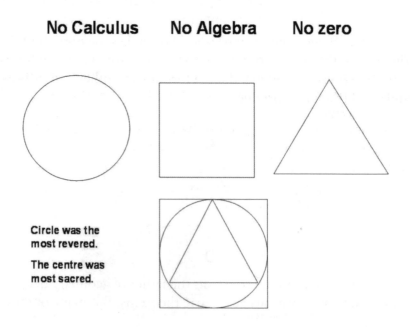

No Calculus   No Algebra   No zero

Circle was the most revered.

The centre was most sacred.

Our ancestors got to know how to use these three geometric figures to great effect. Euclid, the acclaimed Greek philosopher and mathematician who lived around 300 BCE, used the circle for dividing a line exactly in half. He stated that a line of indeterminate length could be divided into two equal parts by constructing two circles, one at each end of the line, both of exactly the same diameter and with a radius larger than half the length of the line. This would result in the two circles overlapping. A vertical line drawn through the two places on the circumference of the circles where they overlapped would bisect the line into two equal parts. It is a method still taught in school geometry lessons today.

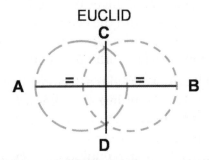

Euclid set out another proposition. If one takes the portion of the original line that falls within the overlapping circles and treats this as the base line of a triangle, then in forming the other two sides an equilateral triangle is produced.

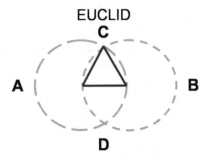

Euclid is sometimes referred to as the father of geometry because he wrote down the various geometric theorems. But many of these concepts were well understood by our ancestors hundreds, even thousands of years before the written word enabled them to be recorded. The idea of the use of two circles for a range of geometric constructions was well known before Euclid recorded its potential. It has been passed down to us as the *Vesica Piscis*.

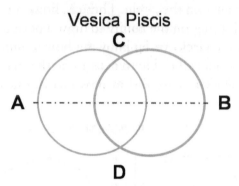

It was the central area where the two circles overlap – the *Vesica* – that was the most sacred. According to tradition, it achieved its sacred status because its shape resembles that of the vulva, the origin of life and therefore seen as the source of creation, the creation of all mankind. However, according to tradition, somewhere along the line of ancestral descent the female sexual connection with this geometric figure became an embarrassment. It was noted that the shape was similar to that of the human eye, so by deftly rotating the image so that the circles were in the vertical plane rather than the horizontal, the eye shape was created. It is believed by some, though it is by no means proven, that this was the origin of the All-seeing Eye.

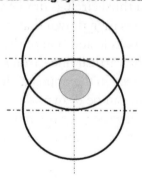

The *all seeing eye* from vesica piscis

As mentioned above, the two circles in the *Vesica Piscis* enabled the construction of a range of geometric figures. Take, for example, the octagon. Most children when studying elementary geometry at school will be taught that the method of constructing an octagon is by using the square and circle method and then describing the octagonal shape within the circle. There is, however, a problem with this method – it relies on the ability to draw a perfect square around the outer edges of circle, or on knowing how to construct a perfect square first in order to be able to determine the exact centre of that square to enable a circle to be drawn so that it touches the edges of the square.

Octagon constructed by square and circle

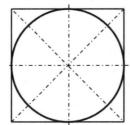 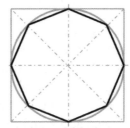

There is another method which is based on the two overlapping circles, drawn in the *Vesica Piscis* about a horizontal axis, illustrated by the line AB in the image shown below. A vertical line is then drawn through the *Vesica* at the points where the circles overlap, line CD, which is at right angles to the horizontal line. At the point where the vertical and horizontal lines cross is the centre of the *Vesica*. From this point a third circle is drawn which just touches the sides of the *Vesica*. A line is then drawn that runs through the centre of the original left-hand circle and one of the two points where the smaller circle touches the vertical line through the *Vesica*, line EF. A similar line can be produced in the opposite direction. Thus the first four sides of the octagon can be drawn.

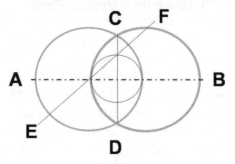

Octagon from Vesica Piscis

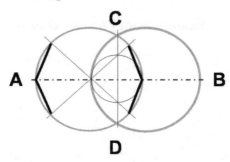

Octagon from Vesica Piscis

To produce the remaining points, draw a circle centred on the centre of the original right-hand circle so that the circumference touches the point of the octagon made by line EF. Now transfer that circle so that its centre is at the point where the side of the octagon is made by line EF, and do the same on the other side of the original circle. The two remaining points of the octagon have now been located on the original left-hand circle, and the octagon can be completed.

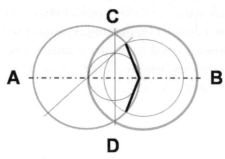

Octagon from Vesica Piscis

Octagon from Vesica Piscis

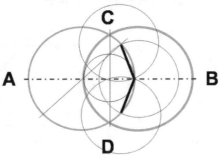

Octagon from Vesica Piscis

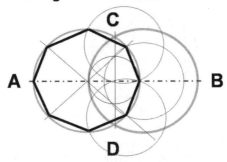

It is easy to envisage that the masons who built incredible structures out of stone would have had a pair of compasses for drawing circles and a square for measuring right angles, both of which are used for marking out patterns on stone, so with just these two tools they could produce a perfect octagon.

Another eight-sided figure which regularly features in religious buildings is the octagram. The same difficulties of producing the octagram from a square and circle apply, exactly the same points on the outer circle needing to be defined. It would seem logical that a mason taught how to produce eight points using the *Vesica Piscis* would use the same technique. There would be only one basic geometric pattern to remember.

Octagram constructed by square and circle

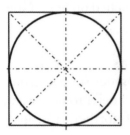 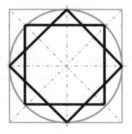

Octagram from Vesica Piscis

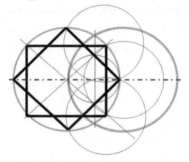

The *Vesica Piscis* provided masons with a range of other tools. For example, earlier in this section attention was drawn to how Euclid defined the equilateral triangle when constructed within the *Vesica*. An equilateral triangle has all its internal angles equal – 60 degrees – so by taking half of the equilateral triangle we can create the angles 90, 60 and 30 degrees. By bisecting each of those angles we can obtain 45, 30 and 15 degrees.

Creating angles in Vesica Piscis

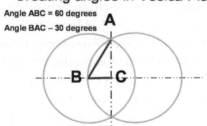

The three most commonly used angles = 90, 60 & 30

The versatility of this simple combination of two overlapping circles creating the *Vesica Piscis* provided an encyclopaedia of knowledge that we have only just touched on here. Now we come to the reason for doing so.

Knights, Architecture and Designs

Throughout the period of the Crusades several groups of knights were formed. Amongst these were the Teutonic knights, who came mainly from the Germanic areas of northern Europe; the Knights Hospitallers, who derived their name from providing hospitals and sanctuaries for pilgrims travelling to and from the Holy Land; and the Knights Templar, whose declared role was to protect pilgrims along the roads leading to the Holy Land, and to Jerusalem in particular. The most prominent of these groups was, without doubt, the Knights Templar, or to give them their full name – The Poor Knights of Christ and the Temple of Solomon. Although they have passed into history as a controversial group, they left a great legacy in architecture, based on the geometric symbolism we have just touched on.

Following the collapse of the Western Roman Empire, Europe entered a period that many historians refer to as the Dark Ages. The Roman Church through its hierarchy of bishops and kings effectively ruled Europe. Therefore, to deviate from the path that the Church dictated was branded as sacrilegious, blasphemous and heretical. Perpetrators could be seized and cast into jails operated by the bishops. As mentioned earlier, the power of the bishops grew. As it did, many were granted titles of nobility. The result was that progress in the west virtually stopped. New discoveries were discouraged; new philosophies were condemned before they could gather any momentum. It was a state of affairs that hung over Europe until the 17th century when the period of the Enlightenment began, primarily in the Protestant countries that had substantially shaken themselves free of the domination of the Roman Church.

In the early 600s CE, a new religion – Islam – had been founded at Mecca by Mohammed. Islamic teaching implies that Islam is not a new religion in the sense that it departs from all the basic philosophies of the older established religions, but is a return to the teachings of Abraham and Moses. It considers that Christianity and Judaism are corruptions of that original religion.

Islam had a very difficult beginning, not unlike the early days of Christianity. Followers of Islam were persecuted, and there were wars both against and in support of it. As Islam spread throughout the Arab world so a new quest for knowledge evolved and a range of scientific, medicinal and mathematical philosophies developed. Whilst the western world was held back by the dogma of Christianity promulgated by the Roman Church, Islamic philosophers bounded ahead. The Arab world became very advanced relative to Western Europe. The period of history known as the Crusades brought the two cultures into a head-on clash. It could be said that the Arabs won the battles, but Europe won the benefits – the benefits of Arabic knowledge. From then on their fortunes reversed: Western Europe moved gradually forward whilst progress in the Islamic world slowed.

One of the major advantages that transferred to Western Europe was the Arabic numbering system – 1, 2, 3, 4, 5, 6, 7, 8, 9 – as a replacement for the cumbersome Roman numerals based on letters, such as DCXIV. As several historians point out, it is so much easier to add up a column of figures using Arabic characters and get the correct answer than doing the same sum using Roman numerals.

As the Crusades progressed, there was a need to rebuild fortifications that had been damaged, to build new castles, bridges, aqueducts, tunnels and other structures in stone. Amongst all the people that were taken prisoner were many skilled craftsmen, including masons. Some of these masons were transferred back to Europe where they became engaged in building a range of structures. Thus it was that the Knights Templar, in particular, who seem to have become acquainted with much of the sophisticated geometry that had been the domain of the Arabs. A patron of the Templars had been Abbot Bernard of Clairvaux, later to be known as St Bernard. At the start of the Second Crusade Bernard had been involved in drawing up the Rule of the Knights Templar, so he had very close contact with them, especially their hierarchy. Various historians credit Bernard with the development of the concept of Gothic architecture based on geometric design knowledge the Templars had acquired from the masons they captured in Palestine. In particular, one concept seems to have captivated them more than any other: the geometry of the two circles in the configuration known as the *Vesica Piscis*, mentioned above. It is from the shape of the *Vesica* that the Gothic arch is derived.

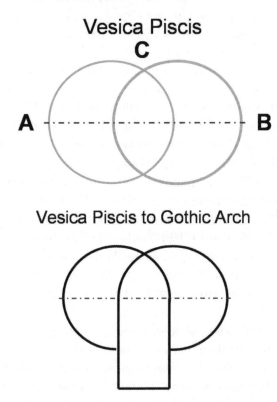

The design is carried through several overlapping circles in the *Vesica Piscis* form. Wonderful examples of this pattern and its significance can be seen in the cathedrals of Canterbury and Peterborough and in the Knights Templar Round Church just off

Fleet Street in London. In Peterborough Cathedral a large area of the interior south wall has this *Vesica* connection carved in it, whilst at the Templar Church it extends around an upper gallery.

Knights Templar – Gothic Arch

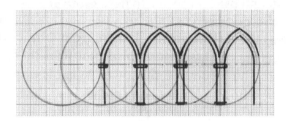

The great cathedral of St Denis just north of Paris was constructed under the direction of Abbot Suger around 1130 CE. In earlier times St Denis had been the burial place for a number of Merovingian kings, later becoming a major church for the Carolingians. The Merovingians were descended from the Goths whom the Romans regarded as barbarians. It was in the 16th century that a prominent architect and artist of that time labelled the style as barbaric. A connection with the Goths was made and hence the term 'Gothic' was created. Most of the great cathedrals of Europe achieved their architectural prominence in the 12th, 13th and 14th centuries and in no small measure this was due to the Knights Templar.

Whilst we have demonstrated how the concept of the *Vesica Piscis* influenced the Gothic style of architecture and the role the Knights Templar played in it, the *Vesica* itself cannot be ignored. It has continued to feature prominently in religious iconography. Around 1100 CE, just a few decades prior to the introduction of the Gothic style at the church of St Denis, the *Vesica* made a dramatic appearance in the altarpiece at Aachen Cathedral. The altarpiece was donated by the Holy Roman Emperor. A few hundred miles away at Chartres the cathedral also prominently displays the *Vesica*, above the main west door. There is a striking similarity between the two images.

In almost every major cathedral in Europe the symbol of the *Vesica* appears somewhere, whether as illustrated above or in stained-glass windows. There is, of course, always the allusion to it in the shape of the Gothic arches.

Aachen Cathedral offers another surprise. The main part of the church built by Charlemagne is circular. Around the centre are eight supporting pillars in octagonal form that lead the eye up to the sacred octagon high above in the tower. What is very striking from the plan view is how the supporting arches lend themselves towards the design of a *cross pattée*, the design of cross later used by the Teutonic knights and in later German military orders such as the Iron Cross. The use of the circle as a basis for the cathedral design is quite obvious. The points of the floor plan octagon would themselves have been equi-spaced and set on a circle. The Iron Cross – *cross pattée* – has slightly curved sides which may well be a function pointing out the link between the eight-pointed cross and the octagon derived from the circle.

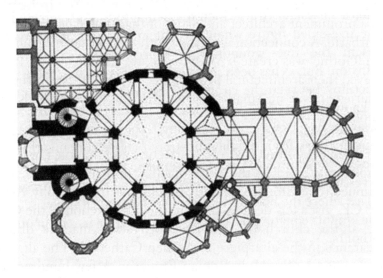

Courtesy of the Tourist Department, Aachen, Germany

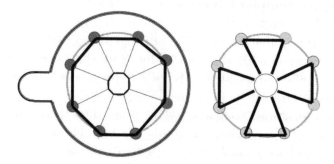

There is also one other aspect of the design of Charlemagne's cathedral which is worth noting, namely the close link between the design at Aachen, the basilica built in Jerusalem over the alleged site of the tomb of Christ, and the churches built by the Knights Templar 300-400 years after Charlemagne's reign. That brings us to the Tudor Rose seen in the replica of King Arthur's Round Table in Winchester.

In many churches dating from the Middle Ages one can find window tracery that is five-sided, imitating the pattern of a pentagram enclosed by a circle. The circle is significant as an ancient geometric character from which the pentagram can be created.

The five-sided figure when present in a church is believed to represent the five wounds that Christ suffered during his Crucifixion. But, as has been seen earlier in this section, there is also a direct link between the circle and the creation of the geometric form known as the *Vesica Piscis* which in turn is the basis of what we know as Gothic architecture. In many respects, the representation of King Arthur's Round Table illustrated above contains the same themes as the Church of the Holy Sepulchre: the circular exterior; the five-sided figure of the Tudor rose at the centre representing the place where the body of Christ is buried; the 24 places set aside for the knights equating to the earth revolving on its axis in one day of 24 hours.

The Knights Templar Churches

In 1118, the Knights Templar officially became a force to be reckoned with, under the privilege of papal protection. In addition to being credited with the development of the Gothic style of architecture, they proceeded to build a large number of churches, most of them circular. It is estimated that in England alone there may have been some 70 such churches. Ruins have been located in several parts of the country, including the foundations of one that was discovered in Dover in the late 19th century. It is hardly surprising that the town should have had one, this being the closest port for access to the European continent. Today there are only four such churches left that are in regular use: Temple Church in London; Cambridge; Northampton; and Little Maplestead in Essex.

The church in Cambridge is particularly well documented and accessible. Although known locally simply as the Cambridge Round Church, its correct title is the Church of the Holy Sepulchre and it was built around 1135, some 17 years after the Templars received their papal rule.

One of the key influential characters in the formation of the Knights Templar is cited as Hugues de Payen. He is known to have been a cousin of the Count Hugh of Champagne and was therefore strongly associated with the nobility of that period. Some historians refer to him as Count Hugues de Payen implying that he held a noble title. According to genealogical records, it would seem that Hugues de Payen was, nevertheless, descended from Charlemagne through the Emperor Louis I, the Pious, and Charles II, the Bald, King of the West Franks. It would be unlikely, therefore, that he would have been unaware of the cathedral at Aachen, or who built it. After the First Crusade it seems that Hugues de Payen persuaded Count Hugh to make a gift to the Abbot Bernard of some land at Clairvaux on which to build a monastery. Hugues de Payen, therefore, had strong connections with the ruling nobility of the day, credentials as a descendant of Charlemagne, as well as influential ecclesiastic connections, all of which must have been of some benefit to his becoming the first Grand Master of the Knights Templar, an

Order credited with inspiring Gothic architecture. It does not then seem coincidental that the round churches of England follow a style employed by Charlemagne at Aachen. Furthermore, they contain similar symbolism.

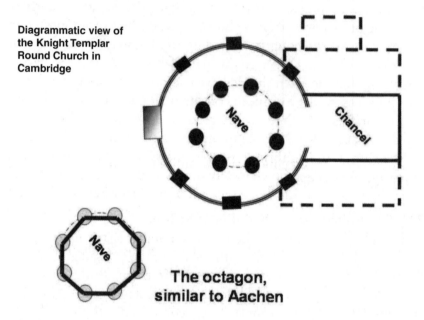

Diagrammatic view of the Knight Templar Round Church in Cambridge

Nave

Chancel

The octagon, similar to Aachen

Nave

An interesting feature common to both Aachen Cathedral and Cambridge Round Church is that the circle on which the pillars sit is exactly half the diameter of the circle that forms the outer walls. This in turn lends itself to the construction of yet more geometrical figures. Just two are illustrated opposite:

Geometrically produced eight-pointed star

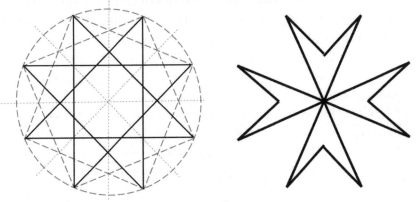

The *crux forchette* is the more significant of the two. It is the symbol of the Knights of St John.

The Symbolism of the Knights of St John

The knights of St John and the Knights Templar share many aspects of medieval history and links with the era of the Crusades. The *crux forchette* and the *cross pattée* are amongst them. Both are eight-pointed and can be derived from the sacred octagon – the symbol of eternity. The octagram is most closely connected with them. As was seen in the earlier diagram, this too can be derived from the octagon and as such has eight points.

The Knights of St John are closely linked with the island of Malta. There are two wonderful cathedrals on the island, one at Mdina and the other in the centre of Valletta.

When St Paul was undertaking his journeys around the Mediterranean on his missionary work to spread the gospel of Christ, one of the islands he is recorded as having visited was Malta. The boat on which he was sailing was shipwrecked in a storm off the coast of the island, but he and his companions managed to get safely ashore. They made their way inland, set up camp and settled down to an evening around a fire. According to tradition, when Paul was collecting wood for the fire, he was bitten by a poisonous snake as he bent down to pick up a branch. Although made ill by the bite, Paul survived and attributed his survival to God answering his prayers. When he had recovered, Paul is credited with having converted the Roman governor of the islands to Christianity. Again according to tradition, the cathedral at Mdina is supposedly built on the site of the house of that Roman governor, which was near the site of Paul's encampment. The present cathedral is a mere 400 years old and supersedes an earlier church that was destroyed by an earthquake. It is as if the symbolism of the circle described by its dome is a representation of the Earth, the dwelling place of man, whilst high above is the sacred octagon, symbolising the eternity of Heaven. The image of the *crux forchette* has been incorporated into the pavement in front of the cathedral.

The cathedral in Valletta is known as St John's Co-Cathedral. Until the 19th century the see of the bishop was based in Mdina. In the early 19th century he was also permitted to use St John's, although its primary role was as a church for knights. It therefore adopted the dual role of church and seat of the bishop, hence the name Co-Cathedral.

Within the architecture of St John's we find not only the sacred octagon, this time in a circular ceiling against which the eight segments are ornately decorated, but also the octagram. It appears in copious quantities. Similarly, the same image is found at the cathedral in Mdina, decorating pillars and ceiling alike.

What we see from all of this is that knights were not just warriors. Clearly at the higher levels of the organisation there was an understanding and respect for a range of symbols and meanings that were attached to them. One can only imagine that the more junior members amongst their ranks would in time be taught their significance, a significance which in their world may have brought them closer to the deity, as recognised through the spiritual association with the concept of creation and how everything appeared to have a purpose. Some of that symbolism was part of their uniform, the *crux forchette* and the *cross pattée* being two examples. Through examples such as the octagram we see a close association with the eight points of the sacred octagon and hence symbolically a reference to eternity. So simple yet so effective a message.

[Author's note: A high proportion of the observations made in this section are the consequence of the many years of research, travel and deliberation I undertook in respect of another subject. As so often happens when investigating one thing, something else crosses one's path. I had lived in Cambridge for several years and had been intrigued by the circular design of the Church of the Holy Sepulchre. Later I had made a discovery in relation to the way that the sun appeared to have been aligned with key features of the church and presented those findings in an earlier work – The Secrets of Solomon's Temple. *I have long held the view that, whenever possible, I should try and visit the places where events from history that I am writing about actually took place. It was as I was taking an interest in Aachen Cathedral, and visited it because of the association with Charlemagne, that I noted the comparison between the circular design of the cathedral and that of the Knights Templar round churches built some 300 years later. Despite making numerous enquiries and referring to various academic works, including a search of possible sources in the library of the Royal Institute of British Architects (RIBA) in London, I have not located any material that makes any such comparison or connection. I have found that truly astonishing. That the Knights Templar should have viewed it as a design worth replicating, not only in the UK but elsewhere in Europe, implies a very deep symbolic connection that they understood. That the concept of the circular churches like those in Cambridge and London appears to have been based on the design of the oldest cathedral in Europe, one built by the acknowledged first Emperor of the Holy Roman Empire, suggests that those who undertook the original design – most probably the master masons who built it – saw something symbolically significant in it. Clearly that design must have been explained to Charlemagne before he found the funds for work to start, and he must have been sufficiently enthusiastic about the symbolism of the design to give the go-ahead*

for building work to be undertaken. Noting that the founding father of the Knights Templar would seem to have been descended from Charlemagne, and the vast array of books and academic works that have been published on the subject of Templar history and mythology, I find it, yet again, astonishing that this connection does not seem to have been explored in depth by anyone. If it has been, it is not obvious.]

Section 6

Prominent Knights of Old

Having looked at the origin of the knights, the historic setting of their rise, the Orders to which many belonged, and some of the symbolism attached to their culture, it seems appropriate to consider the deeds of just a few Knights of Old. These were not men with fictional names like Sir Lancelot or Sir Galahad, whose deeds are so well known that merely uttering their names brings forth images long imprinted in the memory. They have not received the widespread adulation that comes from having been recorded in poetical verse. They were not the son of a monarch to be recorded in royal portraits, family paintings or tapestries, or immortalised in plays, like the Black Prince – son of Edward III, for example. These were, in theory, men of lesser standing, whose names will not have been mentioned in great detail in history books; they have appeared in only the footnotes of history. Nevertheless, through their lives they left a story worth telling.

The stories surrounding the knights mentioned have been selected because of their variety. They each lived in about the same period, and in some instances, their lives or events that were associated with them, overlapped. To put them and the events into context it is worth setting out other historical events that were taking place in their era, especially as they affect the English Crown.

There is an old expression that blood is thicker than water, which implies that family ties are important. But when kingship and nobility were at stake there were many instances when such a concept quickly evaporated. Power, position and wealth were what mattered. Family rivalry for power could result in wars; sisters were known to murder brothers; brothers would murder brothers to improve their chances of inheritance; sons would openly challenge their fathers in an effort to seize a crown.

William the Conqueror to the Anarchy

William the Conqueror had nine children, five girls and four boys. Of the girls, Adeliza is believed to have been promised in marriage to Harold of England – who was ultimately defeated at the Battle of Hastings in 1066 by her father – when she was still very much a child. She may have died in 1065, though some accounts suggest she went into a convent and died after the year 1100. Cecily joined a convent to become an Abbess. Agatha was to have married Alfonso VI of Castile, but died during the journey from Normandy to her marriage. Constance married the Duke of Brittany and is believed to have been murdered a few years later by being poisoned. The priority in inheritance went to the boys in the order of their birth; Robert, Richard, William and Henry. Richard was killed in a hunting accident in the New Forest some 12 years before William I died, and was buried in Winchester Cathedral. Thus, the kingdom in England and Normandy was divided between William's surviving sons. Robert was to inherit Normandy and the associated titles including Duke of Normandy; his second son, William, would become King of England; the third surviving son would not inherit any titles, but was left most of the money.

With the death of William I – the conqueror, power became paramount and there was no love lost between the siblings as they manoeuvred to consolidate their respective positions.

Robert Curthose (1053-1134) became Duke of Normandy in the year 1087 when William I died, but being the eldest he believed he should inherit all the titles, including being King of England. Several supporters of Robert from noble families attempted to dislodge his brother William Rufus from the crown of England but failed. Robert had very little money after the failed attempt against William, so he sold a large area of Normandy to his younger brother Henry Beauclerc. William then invaded Normandy, forcing a peace settlement between himself and Robert. They then embarked on a joint campaign against their younger brother, defeating and forcing him to hand back most of the lands in Normandy that he had bought from Robert. A few years later, Robert went off on the First Crusade and was present at the capture of Jerusalem in the year 1099. He returned to Normandy the following year.

William II (Rufus) took part in several wars involving Normandy, France, the Scots and the Welsh between the years 1087 and 1100, and to pay for them he imposed heavy taxes on the people of England. This made him very unpopular throughout the country. In 1100 – the year his brother Robert returned to Normandy – William Rufus was killed in a hunting accident in the New Forest when an arrow fired by Walter Tyrell apparently ricocheted from a tree and into William's chest. As Tyrell was then seen to ride off at great speed, there has been much speculation that it was no accident but yet another attempt by Robert and his supporters to seize the throne of England. Ironically, as William did not have any sons, the crown of England now passed to the third and youngest brother, Henry Beauclerc.

Henry Beauclerc became King Henry I of England when his older brother, William Rufus, was killed. Most people in England had expected his older brother, Robert, to gain the throne. The centre of the court in England at that time was at Winchester, which was also where the treasury was kept. Henry seized his opportunity and rushed to Winchester to capture the treasury, without which the country could not operate, and declared himself King of England. Robert was incensed when he heard what Henry had done. He assembled an army and in the year 1101 sailed to Portsmouth, but Henry had had sufficient time to secure his own forces and was able to stop Robert. In the end, Robert realised that he would not win, so withdrew to Normandy. Henry then married Edith, the daughter of Malcolm III, King of Scotland, which provided a period of peace between the two countries.

Henry realised that he could not trust his older brother not to continue to attempt to try and seize the throne of England which he obviously coveted. So, in the year 1106, Henry invaded Normandy, captured his brother and imprisoned him in the Tower of London, before moving him to Devizes, Bristol and Cardiff. Robert spent the next 28 years as a prisoner until his death at Cardiff in the year 1134, after which he was buried in Gloucester Cathedral. Thus the youngest surviving son of William the Conqueror, who was left a little money but no titles, ultimately succeeded to all the titles of England and Normandy that his father had achieved, and all the money.

Henry I had many children, most of whom were illegitimate and therefore not in contention to inherit the crown of England. He had two legitimate children that he recognised: his son William Adelin (Athling), and his daughter Matilda (sometimes known as Maud). William drowned in a shipping accident off the coast of France in the year 1120. This left Henry's daughter as his only recognised heir.

But on Henry's death, William the Conqueror's daughter Adela, sister to Robert, William Rufus and Henry, now provided the king. Whilst her two older brothers, Robert and William Rufus, were squabbling between themselves and causing problems for her other brother, Henry, Adela had married the eldest son of the Count of Blois. Her husband, Stephen, was therefore the brother-in-law to each of William the Conqueror's sons. In due course, as a result of her marriage, she became the Countess of Blois, Chartres and Meaux and a member of one of the wealthiest families in France. She and Stephen had eleven children, of whom ten survived childhood. When Robert decided to join the First Crusade Stephen went as well, returning to France briefly in the year 1100. He rejoined the Crusades the following year, but was killed at the first Battle of Ramla, commanded by King Baldwin I of Jerusalem. Adela ran all the family estates whilst her husband was away and her children were growing up. She seems to have had a good relationship with her brother, Henry I, and made arrangements for her son, also called Stephen, then a teenager, to join him at the English court. This paved the way for Stephen, a grandson of William the Conqueror, to gain the throne. Amongst her other children who found success in England was Henry of Blois. He was raised at Cluny Abbey and went on to become Abbot of Glastonbury Abbey and Bishop of Winchester.

Stephen of Blois, King of England, was about 40 years of age when Henry I died. He had been in Henry's court for some years and was close to his uncle. Henry had previously named his daughter Matilda as his heir and had also ensured that all the barons in his kingdom supported that intention and swore allegiance to her. Stephen claimed that on his deathbed Henry had named him as his successor, and therefore seized the crown of England. However, there were other contenders, the main one being his cousin Matilda (Maud) whom he had usurped. The other was Stephen's older brother, Theobald, who had become Count of Blois, Chartres, Champagne and Brie. As the older brother he had more right to the throne than Stephen but decided not to contest it. Any other possible contenders were of illegitimate birth and therefore not deemed suitable. Matilda, however, was not prepared to give up her claim so easily. This resulted in a period of civil war known as The Anarchy.

Matilda (Maud) was the oldest surviving child of Henry I, and grand-daughter of William the Conqueror. Matilda's first husband was the Germanic King Henry V, who became King of the Romans and Holy Roman Emperor. Thus Matilda became the Empress. She and her husband had no children. Her husband died in the year 1125, some ten years before her father, but Matilda did not remain a widow for long. She married Geoffrey of Anjou, with whom she had three sons: Henry, Geoffrey and William. Henry would later become King Henry II of England.

[Author's note: The Anarchy – the succession crisis that lasted 19 years, 1135-1154.

Although Matilda's cousin Stephen had become king with the support of the barons, he soon alienated many of them. He also irritated his younger brother, Henry of Blois, the Bishop of Winchester, by arresting a number of bishops. Matilda meanwhile had gained the support of her uncle, the King of Scotland, who attacked England from the north, although not with any great vigour. One of the illegitimate contenders for the throne was

Matilda's half-brother Robert, Earl of Gloucester. Robert had originally given his support to Stephen, but when Matilda arrived in England and established a base at Arundel Castle in Sussex he switched sides in support of his sister. Stephen attacked Lincoln Castle, but was surrounded by Matilda's army. He was captured and imprisoned in Bristol. Matilda then went to London to rule the country, but later moved to Oxford Castle. Stephen's wife, also named Matilda, raised support for her husband and attacked Winchester. During this battle Robert, Earl of Gloucester was captured and held prisoner. Matilda negotiated for the return of her brother. This resulted in a settlement that included the reinstatement of Stephen to the throne. However, the Anarchy was only fully concluded by the Treaty of Wallingford. By this treaty, Stephen acknowledged Matilda's eldest son, Henry of Anjou, as being the rightful heir to the throne, but it was agreed that Stephen would remain king until his death. Thus, in due course, Matilda's son, and great grandson of William the Conqueror, became Henry II King of England.

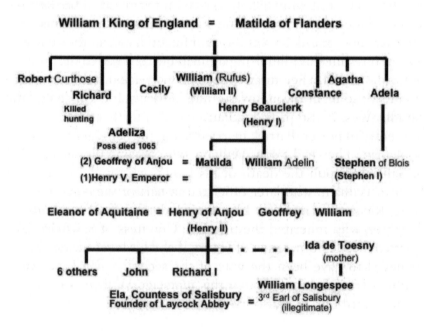

William Longespee, Earl of Salisbury, and Sir William II Longespee

In Salisbury Cathedral there are two tombs on the lids of which are carved almost identical images. They represent a father and son from a once noble family. Both are portrayed as knights dressed in armour, complete with sword and shield. The father is buried in the cathedral, whilst the tomb for the son is empty.

The title Earl of Salisbury was created, forfeited, declared dormant or extinct, and restored on no fewer than five occasions from the mid-12th century through to the 17th century. William Longespee, third Earl of Salisbury, was a member of the family for whom the title was originally created around the year 1150.

The first earl was Patrick of Salisbury. Like the first Earl of Warwick who had been the constable of that town, Patrick had been the constable of Salisbury. Although highly regarded and with considerable power and connections that the role of constable provided him, he was not a noble. He had a sister whom he encouraged to marry John FitzGilbert, the marshal to King Stephen. The role of marshal has been interpreted to be both the keeper of the king's horses and the head of the soldiers who made up the royal bodyguard, so was a very influential role at the centre of power. It resulted in John being ultimately promoted to the position of Lord Marshal, a hereditary title. The marriage of his sister was to result in the birth of one of the most charismatic knights of the Middle Ages. It also provided Patrick with a further connection to the centre of power. Patrick married Sybil, the daughter of a minor nobleman. They had a son, William, who became the second Earl of Salisbury upon the death of his father, who was murdered in France. William, who later officiated in part of the coronation of King Richard I, married Eleonore and they had one child, a daughter, who inherited the title Ela, Countess of Salisbury. She married the illegitimate son of Henry II and his lover Ida de Toesny (believed to have been the wife of the second Earl of Norfolk), William Longespee. Through this marriage William Longespee became third Earl of Salisbury.

William had an illustrious career in the service of King John until the sealing of the Magna Carta. He was a consummate warrior, leading armies into battle in several wars across Europe. When King John died, the throne passed to Henry III, who was only nine years of age. William is credited with having assisted the regency that followed. During the regency William also encountered Hubert de Burgh who had also been a strong ally of King John and had received a number of prestigious positions and titles as a consequence. It is alleged that there was a great rivalry between William and de Burgh during the regency that resulted in William being poisoned by de Burgh. William was buried in Salisbury Cathedral. In a book of unusual facts about Salisbury and its cathedral there is mention that in the 18th century, William's tomb was opened and inside was found the skull of the skeleton as well as the remains of a dead rat which, on further examination, showed signs of having eaten something that contained arsenic.[76] This adds some weight to the story of the de Burgh poison.

William II of Salisbury was the eldest child of Ela, Countess of Salisbury, and William, third Earl of Salisbury. For reasons that are unclear, William II did not gain the earldom. Indeed it seems that he was dispossessed of his inheritance by Henry III. In a letter to Pope Innocent IV he is noted as stating:

> '...for the King of England, my kinsman and liege lord, hath bereft me of the title earl and of that estate, but this he did judiciously, and not in displeasure...' [77]

Although he had been disinherited of the title of earl, he was still permitted to assume the title of a knight and enjoyed eminently influential connections that permitted him to make direct contact with the Pope. From such a contact in the year 1247 he seems to have inspired sufficient confidence to receive a grant of assistance, for he was then able to raise 200 mounted warriors (knights) to join him on a further crusade, the seventh, which was led by Louis IX of France.

Egypt was seen as a key to defeating the Muslim armies and recapturing the city of Jerusalem that been lost for the second time a few years earlier. Having assembled his army, Louis IX set sail for Damietta, a port on the Nile delta which was already occupied by crusaders from an earlier invasion. Most of the former occupants of Damietta had fled and established a new fortified town on the banks of the Nile at Al-Mansurah. It was here that a major battle took place. In front of Al-Mansurah was a canal. Louis's crusaders arrived on one bank, with the defenders on the opposite side. So the first task was to find a way across. With the assistance of someone who knew the area well, a shallow area was located and a section of the army was able to cross.

A major chronicler of the time was a monk from St Albans by the name of Matthew Paris. In respect of the Battle of Al-Mansurah he states that there were bitter disputes between the Templars and Hospitallers throughout the era of the crusades and these surfaced again prior to the battle. Robert of Artois – brother of Louis IX – had apparently inflamed them by urging them into battle before the rest of the army arrived. The Masters of the Templars and Hospitallers resisted, believing it was better to wait for the main force before taking action. Robert of Artois accused them of being half-hearted and suggested that they were primarily interested in making money, having a quiet life, and fighting between themselves for control over territory and events. He is believed to have stated that it was because of the conflict between the two Orders that the crusades had not been so successful in the past in winning territory and keeping it. The Masters of the Orders retaliated. In the heat of the argument that followed, William Longespee intervened, cooling inflamed tempers and bringing order to the situation. By the second week of February 1250, hundreds of knights led by William II Longespee (of Salisbury), Knights Templar and Knights Hospitallers, were assembled and ready for battle, although the main crusader force had still to arrive from Damietta. All the Orders engaged the Egyptians in battle. To the surprise of the knights, the gates of the town were suddenly opened and, believing it was all but deserted, the knights rushed in. It was, however, an elaborate trap. Once within the walls of the town, and unable to manoeuvre easily, they were attacked vigorously by the Egyptian defenders. Robert of Artois and William Longespee II having been dislodged from their horses apparently sought refuge in a house, but were soon discovered, overcome and killed. According to Matthew Paris, two Templars, one Hospitaller and one other knight escaped alive from the aftermath of the battle. Hundreds of knights must have been killed in this one engagement.

The crusaders retreated to their camp on the other side of the canal, and fortified their position with walls and ditches. A few days later, Muslim forces attacked the camp and the shiploads of food and reinforcements that were being transported from Damietta along the Nile. Under siege, food and water were quickly exhausted and many in the army became sick. Louis IX tried to negotiate a settlement. The Egyptians were not prepared to agree terms. This led to the crusaders trying to make a desperate retreat under cover of darkness in April 1250, back to Damietta. The Muslim army followed, engaged the crusaders in battle when they were weakened, and almost annihilated them. King Louis IX was captured along with his brothers and held for ransom. He was later released and returned to France, having agreed not to take part in any future crusades. It is believed that Louis withdrew with some 12,000 crusaders who had been made prisoners from this and earlier battles, but they left behind up to 30,000 dead crusaders.

Two years later, the remains of William Longespee II were released by the sultan and carried to Acre. He was buried in the church of St Cross. The tomb and commemorative effigy were erected in Salisbury Cathedral by his family.

John FitzGilbert and his son, William the Marshal

John FitzGilbert was a colourful character of his time. The word 'Fitz' was a means of indicating that the man was not of legitimate birth. He lived at a time when England, or rather the crown of England, was in some turmoil. Following the Norman conquest led by William I, Duke of Normandy, there was a period of around 100 years of dispute between factions in England and France for the ownership and governance of lands on both sides of the English Channel. Added to all this were the political manoeuvrings within the Holy Roman Empire, the whole being set against the background of the Crusades. To put John FitzGilbert and his son, William the Marshal, in context it is worth examining what had been happening with the crown of England and influencing events taking place in the background, hence the opening sequence in this section entitled 'William the Conqueror to the Anarchy'.

The Legend of John FitzGilbert

John FitzGilbert was the son of Gilbert Giffard, who was the Marshall to Henry I Beauclerk. FitzGilbert was also employed in the service of Henry I, probably assisting his father. Most likely his duties included tasks like book entries, collecting debts and imprisoning debtors. When his father died or became too infirm to continue, it seems that FitzGilbert took over the full role of Marshall. When Henry I died and Stephen of Blois seized the throne, FitzGilbert continued to serve in the royal household and even accompanied Stephen on trips to Normandy. In his role as Marshall he took possession of two castles in Wiltshire – one at Marlborough, the other at Lugershall – and reinforced them.

When the dispute about the succession to the throne of England erupted between Matilda and Stephen, FitzGilbert remained loyal to Stephen, but it seems he kept a low profile as if not wishing to become closely associated with either side. Some historians note that during this time he also assembled a number of knights who were loyal to him, thereby adding to his personal protection. He clearly saw danger in the events unfolding around him. He also seems to have used the opportunity to enrich himself by raiding and taking control of the properties of those who were supporters of Matilda. When Empress Matilda arrived in England to challenge Stephen, his loyalties began to waiver and he decided to support Matilda.

During the above period, John married Aline Pipard. This seems yet a further move to consolidate his position because records in Wiltshire suggest that Pipard's father was one Walter Pipard, who was Lord of the Manor of Wooton Basset in Wiltshire. Obviously feeling secure at Lugershall castle and a full supporter of Matilda, he began raiding the properties of Stephen's supporters in Wiltshire. One, whose properties John frequently raided were those of Patrick, the Constable of Salisbury, who would later become 1st Earl of Salisbury. After some years of such raids, Patrick, who had supported Stephen – and was a well connected feudal landowner and had accumulated some considerable wealth – persuaded FitzGilbert that he should terminate his marriage to Pipard and marry his sister, Sibyl. This was done. Stephen had been captured and imprisoned in Bristol. Patrick deserted Stephen and worked with FitzGilbert in support of Matilda. Now they were both on the same side and raided any of Stephen's known supporters, thereby increasing their respective wealth still further.

FitzGilbert served Matilda whilst she was at Oxford, and when the Battle at Winchester broke out in the year 1141 between the army Stephen's wife had assembled and Matilda's army led by her half brother, Robert, Earl of Gloucester, FitzGilbert was there. When it became clear that Winchester would fall to Stephen's supporters, FitzGilbert organised to take Matilda to Lugershall Castle, whilst Robert stayed and continued the fight thereby enabling Matilda's escape. In so doing, Robert was captured by Stephen's supporters.

FitzGilbert had six children with Sibyl, four sons and two daughters. His first son was also named John; his second son was named William. With Stephen restored to the throne, there was a conflict between the two men that led to Stephen laying siege to FitzGilbert's castle at Newbury in the year 1152. This was just two years prior to Stephen's death. At one stage, a truce was called. To ensure FitzGilbert honoured his obligations, Stephen took the young William, believed to have been about seven years old, and held him hostage. FitzGilbert completely ignored his obligations. Stephen is believed to have called FitzGilbert to the castle walls and reminded him that he had his son William as a hostage and advised him that if he didn't comply with Stephen's wishes, William would be hung the next day. FitzGilbert is alleged to have responded. 'I have the anvils and the hammer to forge still better sons.' King Stephen did not hang William for had he done so elements of history would have changed dramatically.

The Legend of William the Marshal

Cardinal Langton was Archbishop of Canterbury in the early 13th century from 1207 until 1228 CE. The Crusades were at the mid-point of the 200 year struggle for Papal and Christian control of the Holy Land. It was the era when Europe was awash with the comings and goings of knights of all nationalities as they set out for, and returned from, the battlefields of the Levant. Cardinal Langton is attributed as having described one such knight as being the greatest knight that ever lived. The name of the knight was William the Marshal (also spelt Marechal and Marshall).

William the Marshal began life in the lower orders of nobility, but was to rise to the title of first Earl of Pembroke and earn a reputation as a fierce fighter as well as confidant to three kings of England. His effigy, showing him in full armour, is emblazoned amongst a group of tombs in the floor of the Knights Templar Round Church at the Inner Temple, London.

William was the son of an English nobleman, John FitzGilbert, who, as mentioned above, had been the marshal to King Stephen and supporter of Matilda. John FitzGilbert had married twice; his second wife – descended through the barons of Salisbury – was the sister of Patrick, first Earl of Salisbury. There were several other children in the FitzGilbert family who were older than William. As such, he was unlikely to inherit any titles or property. Whatever he was going to achieve in life, therefore, he had to create for himself. Despite this, his background meant that he was surrounded by other noble families and thereby potential connections.

In common with the customs of the age, as he grew older, probably in his mid-teens, he was sent to work in the household of a prominent nobleman as a squire. In Normandy, in a small town about midway between the ports of Dieppe and Le Havre, his father had a cousin who was a knight and the manager and keeper of the household, a role normally described as a chamberlain. It was here that the young William was sent to learn and absorb the skills required that would ultimately lead to him being made a knight. Even at a young age, William had apparently shown an adept use of the sword, shield and lance and learned martial skills quickly. As a squire, he would have tended horses, learned about their care, how to ride them, mount and dismount in full chain-mail without the aid of a stirrup. The weight of the chain-mail, battle sword and shield would have been difficult enough to manage without the need to fight in life and death struggles that may have lasted several hours, so fitness and bodily strength also needed to be developed. As a squire, he would have also learned the manners and protocol of court where he would encounter noblemen of all ranks, and, of course, the daughters and wives of such noblemen. Etiquette and conversation would be developed, along with an appreciation of such pursuits as singing and an appreciation of religious customs and duties. Several accounts describe him as being tall, around six feet, with a strong physique and a presence that might have suggested he was actually the emperor.

At the time William was in Normandy as a squire learning his skills, the English king was Henry II, the Empress Matilda's eldest son. For most of his time, Henry lived in that part of his kingdom that is today a large area of north-east France. Indeed amongst Henry's titles he was King of England, Count of Anjou, Duke of Normandy, Duke of Aquitaine, Duke of Gascony, Count of Nantes, and Lord of Ireland. He was born in Le Mans, lived mainly at Chinon in the Loire Valley, and on his death was buried at Fontevrauld Abbey in the district of Anjou, close to Chinon. Even his successor as King of England, his son, Richard I – the Lionheart, was buried in the same abbey, as was Henry's wife, Eleanor of Aquitaine. Thus young William was receiving his education in what was the centre of power and governance for England and

Normandy. France at that time was outside of those borders.

In the late 1160s and through the early 1170s, there were a series of conflicts that broke out between Henry II and the King of France, who tried to gain control over parts of Normandy. William's mentor, John FitzGilbert's cousin, as a knight himself was obliged to join the fight against France. William was supposedly about seven years old in the year 1152 when he was held hostage by Stephen, so he would have been in his early to mid-twenties when these conflicts erupted. One such conflict was in the year 1167 when William was aged 21. He apparently rode with his mentor – the chamberlain. As a squire he would not have been expected to take part in the fight, but to mind the chamberlain's possessions, care for the horses, repair broken equipment, prepare food for his master and guard any prisoners captured in the field of battle. That changed, however, at a village named Drincourt which is today the town of Neufchatel-en-Bray near the city of Rouen.

On the evening prior to the battle, William was dubbed a knight by the Lord of Tancarville and as a gift in celebration he was given a fine war-horse. For a young man without possessions of land and titles this must have been the highlight of his life so far.

The next day saw the battle for Drincourt, and the recently dubbed new knight fought hard and well. At one time he was surrounded by men from the opposing force supporting the French king. William had been dragged from his horse by a form of grappling hook used by an opposing knight. He managed to fight his way out of the town, but the horse he had been given only the evening before died from its wounds. William had his knightly honour, but was without a horse and, as a squire, did not have the financial means to buy another. With this being his first engagement he had not appreciated a fine detail: not only should one fight, but if the opportunity arose one should capture war-horses that might be available. They were valuable as a trading commodity and hence provided a means of financial independence.

After the battle, a tournament was organised. William, having lost his own horse in the battle, was able to borrow one through his mentor and thereby enter. At that time, a tournament usually consisted of four elements, each designed to show prowess with a knightly weapon, provide training for knights, and a display of horsemanship. Two of the elements were feats of a single knight against a single knight, but there were also group competitions where knights supporting one lord would fight against an equal number of knights supporting another.

About the time when William was first knighted, changes were introduced to the way tournaments were conducted. Prior to that, knightly competitions were almost as brutal as those of the Roman gladiators, where in some cases there was a fight to the death of one of the competitors. In some instances, a fight broke out of the tournament arena and knights chased each other across country, on foot or on horseback, in and out of houses and barns until there was a victor. This type of activity was banned – lords were losing too many good knights and they were expensive and difficult to develop in the first instance. Nevertheless, by the late 12th century, a knight beaten in a tournament might expect to lose all he had. Certainly he would lose his horse and armour, and would have to agree to pay a substantial sum of money as ransom because effectively the beaten knight was a prisoner of the victor. In the later Middle Ages levels of ransom were agreed in advance of the competing knights entering the field, but at the time of William's first tournament, it could mean that the loser had to pay all they had and agree to do so as a bond of honour or their reputations as knights would be sullied forever.

Thus it was that the young William entered his first tournament. He won every competition he entered, beat every opponent he challenged and came away with several war-horses, ransoms and other valuables such as armour that could be sold. Within days, William had transformed from a squire with no land, wealth or title to a knight having value through his victory at the tournament, and a name that would not be easily forgotten, having bested in the field some of the most renowned knights of the day. He entered tournament after tournament and won. On the battlefield he was a strategist as well as an accomplished warrior. He became the celebrity of his time.

Having proved his worth in Normandy, William then transferred to the household of his mother's brother Patrick, who became the first Earl of Salisbury. Patrick had been in Palestine with the crusading armies under Amalric, King of Jerusalem, and William, it seems, had been with him. Guy de Lusignan of Poitou had desires on becoming the King of Jerusalem. Poitou was in the House of Aquitaine of which Eleanor, then married to Henry II of England, was ruler. Guy de Lusignan and his knights were involved in a battle against Patrick and his entourage as they journeyed home. In the fight Patrick was killed; William was injured and taken prisoner for ransom. Eleanor of Aquitaine paid the ransom for William, and Guy de Lusignan was banished from Poitou. Guy de Lusignan was later to become King of Jerusalem and King of Cyprus.

A fact not often dealt with in classroom history is that during the reign of Henry II his young son took responsibility for the throne of England, and as such has become known as the Young Henry. Young Henry's mother was Eleanor of Aquitaine, who had paid the ransom for William to be freed. William was given the opportunity to serve Young Henry, and did so for well over a decade. Acting as tutor and confidant, William taught him much about weapons training and took him to tournaments. Henry became as much a hero of the tournament circuit as William. Some individuals who were due to be made knights preferred to be dubbed by a knight they greatly admired rather than their lord or monarch. Various historians state that Young Henry was made a knight at the hand of his tutor William.

Henry II had agreed the marriage of Young Henry to Marguerite, the daughter of King Louis VII of France, when the children were still less than six years old. The marriage eventually took place at Winchester Cathedral; Young Henry was about 18 years of age and his bride was three years younger. Some ten years after the marriage, William was accused of a romantic entanglement with Marguerite and forced to leave the court. This was later shown to be a false accusation. Young Henry sent his young queen back to her father and recalled William to the court, which perhaps says much about the bond that existed between the two.

As shown with the siblings of William the Conqueror, these ruling families were quite prepared to fight amongst each other for wealth, power and the opportunity to seize a crown or two. Much the same happened with the children of Henry II. Henry ruled three territories – England, Normandy and Anjou – whilst his wife Eleanor was the ruler of Aquitaine. Thus the family ruled a major area of north and western France as well as England. Young Henry had been given little power or rights in the ruling of England or the opportunity to manage the financial affairs of the kingdom. Encouraged by much of the nobility of England, he embarked on a war against his own father. He was supported by his brothers Richard (later known as the Lionheart), John (later to be king) and Geoffrey (Duke of Brittany and Earl of Richmond). Even his mother Eleanor was prepared to fight against her husband, but was captured and imprisoned by Henry before she could join her sons. Young Henry set up an alliance with the King of France, his father-in-law, and the King of Scotland. By defeating their father, the siblings planned to gain control of the territories they felt were their inheritances by splitting up the kingdom. In payment for his support, the King of Scotland would receive a major area of the English counties of Northumberland and Cumberland. This conflict has become known as the Civil War of the years 1173-1174 in which William sided with the Young Henry. Henry II was the victor, but it was a conflict in which many knights on all sides died.

Ten years later, the Young Henry was again at war with his father in northern France. He caught dysentery and died. Most of his knights were hired – what today we would call mercenaries – but William, his loyal friend, was with him. On his death Young Henry asked that his knight's cloak be taken to the Holy Sepulchre in Jerusalem. William fulfilled his wishes and whilst in the Holy Land fought in the Crusades, assisting Guy de Lusignan who was now King of Jerusalem and had been held as a hostage some years previously.

On his return from the Holy Land, William was employed by Henry II, who was now in his late fifties, as one of his knights. This implies that he was impressed with the manner in which he had tutored his son and bore no malice for having fought against him in the 1173-1174 war. However, conflicts with his three remaining sons continued. It is recorded that on one occasion when William and Henry were near Le Mans in northern France heading towards Chinon, Richard spotted his father and thought it an ideal opportunity to capture him. He charged at his father. William seeing this left the other knights guarding the king and charged directly at Richard. William could have killed Richard who had failed to put on his armour. Noting that Richard was not wearing armour and was therefore deemed to be unarmed, instead of killing the king's son, William killed the horse instead, which brought the attempt by Richard to an abrupt halt.

Henry II was pleased at the outcome. Not only had he been saved from an attempted capture by his own son, but that son had not been killed, as he might have been had it been another knight who had challenged Richard. As a reward, Henry arranged a marriage between William and Isabel de Clare, daughter of Richard de Clare, Lord Marshal of England. Henry II died before that arrangement could be honoured. His son, Richard, now inherited the titles he had fought his father – and periodically William as well – for so long to achieve. As the new King Richard I of England, he decided to honour the arrangement that his father had made, and Isabel and William were married in August 1189. Isabel was around 25 years younger than her husband. Through the marriage William received castles and keeps throughout Wales. He was elevated from being a knight and became the first Earl of Pembroke and Striguil, Lord of Leinster, and Lord Marshal of England. In his life he served Young Henry, Henry II, Richard I, John and Henry III as well as fighting in the Crusades and building a formidable reputation on the tournament circuits of England, Normandy and northern France. He and Isabel had ten children. In his role as Lord of Leinster he founded the port and town of New Ross on the River Barrow in County Wexford, Ireland. He also played a major role in the drawing up and sealing of Magna Carta at Runnymede, mediating between King John and the barons. When John died in November

1216, his young son Henry, then aged nine years, inherited the throne of England to become King Henry III. William was elected to be regent, which meant that for many years he was effectively running the country.

Having started his life with few prospects of land or titles and a threat of being hanged by King Stephen, William the Marshal rose to be one of the wealthiest men in England, highly honoured and respected. He left part of his estates to the Knights Templar and in return was buried at the Templar Church in London.

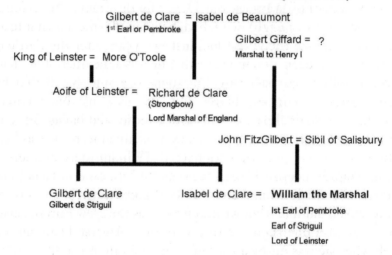

Family tree for William Marshall (Marachel)

Sir Hugh de Hatton

Hugh seems to have had a chain of ancestors extending back to an era prior to the Norman conquest, to noble families in France, through dukes and viscounts. Following the conquest of Britain in the year 1066, various areas of England were allocated to individuals who had been of service to William the Conqueror, either on the battlefield or by some other means.

One such area was centred on Warwick and later became the fief of the Earls of Warwick. In the Middle Ages, such a holder of territory could subdivide an area of land within his fief and allocate it to someone else, perhaps a vassal who had served the earl well. Such gifts were called a feoffment and were land that could be sold by the new holder, rented for others to use, or could be part of an inherited estate.

Thus it seems that one Hugh FitzRichard received a gift of land from William, third Earl of Warwick, in the year 1166, which today is centred on the village of Hatton in Warwickshire. Today Hugh FitzRichard is often referred to as Hugh de Hatton (sometimes written Hewes de Hatton).

The first Earl of Warwick was Henry de Beaumont (he changed his name to Newburgh) who had been made the constable of Warwick Castle in the year 1068, just two years after the Battle of Hastings. The records do not state that he was a member of William of Normandy's original army, but there is a suggestion that his brother took part in the battle. His role as constable involved building a substantial part of the castle's motte and bailey. To have received such a prestigious position as constable means he was held in high regard and was well connected. William the Conqueror's son, William II, became king in the year 1087, but was not a popular ruler. The centre of his court was at Winchester from where he could actively hunt in what we know today as the New Forest. As we saw earlier, on one such hunting trip, on 2 August 1100, he was killed when he was hit by an arrow fired by Walter Tyrell.

Amongst the men that Henry de Newburgh favoured, perhaps as a vassal, was a man who would become Sir Walter of Hatton, Lord of Hatton, and was, it seems, well regarded by William II. Hatton is a village just a few miles outside Warwick, but the lands within the parish were very extensive at the time. Sir Walter's parents are listed as Viscount de Contentin Yvron Bellomontesis and Emma de Bretagne. This suggests a strong Norman connection, perhaps previously known to Henry de Newburgh. Sir Walter had a son, who became Sir Hugh de Hatton, and a daughter, Margery. Sir

Hugh had three sons – Hugh, Roger and Waithew – but it was Hugh who inherited the title and is the subject of this section.

When Hugh de Hatton was born in the year 1110, the papal-inspired First Crusade had been embarked upon and Jerusalem had been in the hands of the Christian armies for ten years. By the time he was 20 years old, the most famous Order of Knighthood, the Knights Templar, had been officially recognised for two years, were expanding rapidly and attracting new recruits, and it is most likely that he joined them. Thus it was that in his early twenties, Hugh de Hatton set out to join the Crusades and to protect the many pilgrims that were heading towards Jerusalem.

Whilst fighting in the Holy Land, Hugh de Hatton was captured and held as a prisoner. It was the usual custom at that time for prisoners of high standing to be ransomed, but that does not seem to have been the case for Hugh. He was imprisoned in Jerusalem for seven years. Legend has it that during his captivity he prayed to St Leonard to secure his release.

St Leonard of Limousin is a rather obscure saint, having supposedly lived in the Frankish kingdom of the early Merovingians during the reign of Clovis in the late fifth century. Although little is known about him, by the 11th century he had developed a remarkable reputation and was attributed with having performed miracles, healing, the safe delivery of a queen during childbirth, and the deliverance of prisoners from captivity. With the latter in mind, it is not surprising that during the Crusades his prowess and abilities grew such that he was one of the most prominent saints of the era, as a result of which numerous churches, abbeys and priories were named in his honour all across Europe.[78]

A fortuitous opportunity enabled Sir Hugh to escape from his captors, though exactly how he achieved this does not seem to be recorded. Free from his trials in prison he made his way back to England. There is then a legend that in his dishevelled state and having aged quite considerably as a result of his captivity, no one would believe him to be the person he said he was. He had apparently married prior to leaving for the Holy Land and had taken a ring and cut it into two pieces. One part was retained by his wife, the other he kept. It was only by showing the part he retained that his wife finally acknowledged him. In recognition and thanksgiving for his escape from captivity, Hugh, who by this time had inherited the knightly title of his father, gave up some 3000 acres of his land and founded a nunnery in the year 1141 (Priory of St Leonard at Wroxall). Sir Hugh's two daughters were intent on joining a religious order and were admitted to the Priory of St Leonard, which was run in accordance with the Benedictine Rule. This abbey flourished until the reign of Henry VIII when, in keeping with the general policy of dissolving the monasteries, Wroxall was closed and progressively demolished. The church, however, was retained and was rededicated as the parish church of St Leonard (Church of England).[79] It later became part of an estate owned by Sir Christopher Wren who refurbished the church. Barely a few stones remain to mark the passing of the abbey, but the church still functions and is today part of a hotel that has been established on the site.

This, then, is the story of a young man who went away to fight as a knight in the Crusades, who was captured and imprisoned, escaped and returned to England, where, to celebrate his gift of freedom, he provided the means for the establishment of a nunnery that then flourished for the next 350 years, dedicated to the saint that had risen to prominence as the deliverer of prisoners from captivity – St Leonard.

Section 7

So it's Good Knight to Chivalry

From all the foregoing information it can be seen that there is much more to the background and concept of 'knights' and 'chivalry' than perhaps many people believe through the popular imagery that has been developed over the centuries.

- It could not have happened without our ancestors having learned to tame horses thousands of years ago, and then designing the harnessing systems that enabled the animals to be ridden and given direction and control. Interestingly, these harnessing systems, some of which existed 7,000 years ago, have changed little except perhaps for minor cosmetic or material developments. This demonstrates how well our ancestors understood the implications and the methodology needed.

- Without the development of the stirrup, the lance, a key weapon of the knights, would have been almost impossible to use – the rider would have fallen from the horse. This led to the greater use of mounted warriors in cavalry units that became the foundation of the organisations of knights that later developed.

- Knights were mounted warriors. Taking that simple definition means that their origins can be traced back probably 3,000 or 4,000 years, although at that time they did not have a defined title.

- Perhaps the earliest identifiable knights had their origins in the Roman Empire. There seems to have been an elite group of mounted warriors, membership of which was open only to privileged families. As well as warriors, they may have been confidential messengers and bodyguards for senior members of the Roman government. Being from selected families who were highly regarded by the administration of the day, and thereby having much to lose, there was a high level of incentive to perform well and to take risks. Loyalty, trustworthiness and obedience would have been hallmarks of their code of operation – the same ideals that came to characterise later Orders of Knighthood.

- It has been interesting to note how one embryonic belief system was seized on in the final century of the disintegrating Roman Empire and used as a means of forging a renewed and re-energised empire built on a combination of military and religious power, the ramifications of which still affect us today.

- With the collapse of the Roman Empire in the west, a power void was left in Europe which led to the forced unification and conquest of large areas of the continent by the Merovingians. They were followed by the Carolingians, and in particular the rise of the charismatic warrior called Charlemagne. It is in his reign that we find the foundations of the feudal system that dominated the Middle Ages, the twin powers of the state and religion, the hierarchy of power that created a concept of the divine right of kings, the structure of noble families and reward systems, the need for noblemen to equip and supply armies in return for their favoured position in society.

- The quest to recover the revered city of Jerusalem on behalf of the Christian religion, and to manage it and the surrounding territory we call the Holy Land, became a focus of intense military activity that lasted for 200 years. During that time various popes, as heads of the only religious faith tolerated in Europe, sanctioned the creation of Orders of Knights out of what had previously been a monastic system. Some of those Orders still exist today, or have influenced the establishment of subsequent Orders that continued to exist until modern times.

- The backgrounds and lives of a small group of individuals who became knights have been recorded. They were, on the one hand, associated with a religious cause. One was sufficiently moved by his experience that on returning to England he provided the means to establish a priory within the monastic orders. We have noted that another went on to be regarded as the one of the finest knights to have received that status. Despite the modest prospects of his early life, he nevertheless went on to be awarded with an earldom.

- Perhaps the most significant point of note is that for so much of the past 1000 years there has been a perpetual struggle between kings and their nobles and knightly supporters to seize the territory controlled by others, even to the point of murdering, fighting or imprisoning their siblings and relatives, just for the purpose of the aggrandisement of themselves and the pursuit of wealth they expected to flow from it. The manner in which many lords and their knights operated was akin to gangster mobs that have characterised some western societies in the past 100 years.

- Through looking at the background of the knights we find that so many aspects of the existence attributed to them and enshrined in legend are almost the opposite of reality. Knights were, in the main, little more than mounted warriors, hired bands of mercenaries and bodyguards for the noble families and kings that employed and obligated them.

- Since the start of the Crusades, Orders of Knighthood have taken particular saints, as nominated by the Roman Catholic Church centuries ago, as their patrons. What is clear, however, is that the deeds these saints are supposed to have performed and that led to their status are as much myth and legend as those of the knights themselves.

- Although literature and other media have encouraged a particular popular impression of the concept of 'chivalry' over the centuries, the reality is somewhat different. Knights were no more than a group of soldiers who undertook a particular role in warfare, having become skilled in using the weapons they had to hand and in employing the military tactics of the period in which they operated. In that sense they were on a par with soldiers in a modern army today. No more and no less.

- The legends of the good knight and the ideals of chivalry that surrounded them appear to have been little more than romantic mythology.

Appendix

Author's Comment on Europe and the Holy Roman Empire
There are several references made in this book to the Holy Roman Empire (HRE) which was effectively created by Charlemagne around 800 CE. This empire, as such, was officially disbanded by Napoleon Bonaparte on 6 August 1806, yet it became clear to me during the research for this book that there are still groups of people perceived to be in high places who harbour some design for its resurrection. No doubt this desire is conceived of some ambition to secure a power, status and wealth they believe they might otherwise have inherited through accident of birth had Napoleon not intervened.

The real influence of the Holy Roman Empire was in the period from 800 CE to around 1500 CE. It was in 1517 CE that Martin Luther embarked on his famous cause for change in the Roman Catholic Church, and in so doing set off a chain reaction that led to the establishment of a new religious structure known as the Reformation. This was followed by a period of about 150 years of wars and conflicts as the Emperor and Roman Catholic Church sought to reinstate their power and influence whilst Protestant groups sought to deny them. The result was that by the middle of the 17th century, the religious map of Europe had substantially altered to the extent that Protestantism dominated the north and west of Europe, whilst Roman Catholicism remained firmly entrenched in the south and east. It is around this time that the era that we know as the Middle Ages came to an end, to be followed by the Renaissance and the Enlightenment.

Following World War 2, a common market policy was established, primarily instigated by France and Germany. Fifty years later, at the start of the third millennium, this had grown to become the European Union. By the end of the first decade of this millennium, the EU has enlarged to include countries that had been part of Eastern Europe in the days when communist political doctrine influenced events in that part of the world.

It is interesting to note how the Europe of Charlemagne and the Holy Roman Empire now coincide to a large extent with the modern European Union. It is as if the Emperor of the HRE has been replaced by an office known as the President of the EU. The difference is that the Emperor was deemed to hold power through blood connection, a hereditary concept, whereas the President is elected.

In addition, there are several organisations that appear to be continuing the ethos of the HRE. One such organisation is called the Reichs College of Princes and Counts of The Holy Roman Empire. It is also known as the Council of Princes. This organisation operates an internet website which purports to list the accredited nobility associated with the HRE in the following European countries: Belgium, Britain, Croatia, France, Germany, Italy, Malta, Poland, Russia and Spain.

Under 'Britain' as at the year 2009, and headed *The Imperial Nobility of Great Britain*, the first name listed is His Serene Highness John George Vanderbilt Henry Spencer-Churchill, 11th Duke of Marlborough, Prince/Furst of Mindleheim (Prince of The Holy Roman Empire). The list then names others associated with such nobility. It is interesting to note that the British royal family are listed with HRE connections, despite the separation of England from the HRE in the reign of King Henry VIII.

[The following has been copied word for word as shown on www. http://imperialcollegeofprincesandcounts.com/_wsn/page3.html]

KINGDOM OF GREAT BRITAIN & NORTHERN IRELAND / ROYAL HOUSE OF WINDSOR

H.M. Queen Elizabeth The Second of The United Kingdom of Great Britain and Northern Ireland
(Princess of The Holy Roman Empire)

H.R.H. The Prince Philip, Duke of Edinburgh
(Prince of The Holy Roman Empire)

H.R.H. The Prince of Wales
(Prince of The Holy Roman Empire)

H.R.H. The Prince William of Wales
(Prince of The Holy Roman Empire)

H.R.H. The Prince Henry of Wales
(Prince of The Holy Roman Empire)

H.R.H. The Prince Andrew, Duke of York
(Prince of The Holy Roman Empire)

H.R.H. Princess Beatrice of York
(Princess of The Holy Roman Empire)

H.R.H. Princess Eugenie of York
(Princess of The Holy Roman Empire)

H.R.H. The Prince Edward, Earl of Wessex
(Prince of The Holy Roman Empire)

H.R.H. Prince James of Wessex, Viscount Severn
(Prince of The Holy Roman Empire)

H.R.H. Princess Louise of Wessex
(Princess of The Holy Roman Empire)

H.R.H. The Princess Anne, Princess Royal
(Princess of The Holy Roman Empire)

H.R.H. Prince Richard, 2nd Duke of Gloucester
(Prince of The Holy Roman Empire)

H.R.H. Prince Edward, 2nd Duke of Kent
(Prince of The Holy Roman Empire)

H.R.H. Prince Michael of Kent
(Prince of The Holy Roman Empire)

H.R.H. Princess Alexandra of Kent
(Princess of The Holy Roman Empire)

COUNTS ARUNDELL OF WARDOUR

Sir Thomas Arundell of Wardour was Created a Count of The Holy Roman Empire by Imperial Letters Patent of the Holy Roman Emperor Rudolph II on 14 December 1595 for capturing the Turkish Standard at the Battle of Gran in the Kingdom of Hungary in the same year. Then formally recognized by King James I by Royal Letters Patent creating him Baron Arundell of Wardour on 4 May 1605. With the death of the 16th and last Baron John Arundell in 1944, the Title of Baron Arundell of Wardour became dormant. The descendants of the 1st Count have the Universal Right to the formal usage of the Titles of Count or Countess of The Holy Roman Empire, being issued within the Imperial Letters Patent concerned. His Imperial and Royal Highness Prince Karl Friedrich of Germany, Duke of Swabia, de jure Emperor Charles VIII I.R., has formally issued an Imperial Decree to ratify the right of claim of all descendants of the body of the 1st Count Thomas Arundell of Wardour of The Holy Roman Empire. Whereas His Imperial Highness has furthermore Conferred and Granted by Imperial Decree and Letters the formal usage of the appellation style and title of Excellency on all descendants of the 1st Count Thomas Arundell of Wardour, who may formally Petition His Imperial Highness, for formal recognition of the Imperial Titles of Count or Countess of The Holy Roman Empire, together with the formal appellation style and Title of Excellency, granted with full rights of Arms. Please see below for the official list of the present Counts of The Holy Roman Empire, who formally hold, bear and enjoy the Title from the first Count Thomas Arundell of Wardour. Persons may be added to this list who have claim to the aforementioned Imperial Title by formal descent of the first Count Thomas Arundell of Wardour. (Counts and Countesses of The Holy Roman Empire under the Title, Rank and Honour of Count or Countess Arundell of Wardour.)

[Author's observation: The term de jure *in the above statement would usually mean lawfully or in accordance with the law. The initials I.R. are interpreted to mean interregnum, a period that notes*

*the time between the end of the reign of one sovereign and the
accession of the next. It has also been pointed out that I.R. may also
mean Imperator Rex – Emperor and King. This, however, is
unlikely as the last official Emperor was Francis, at the time the
HRE was dissolved in 1806 by Napoleon Bonaparte. Emperor
Charles VIII mentioned above, would, under other circumstances,
have been the recipient of that title, and it implies they are waiting
a time when it will be formally restored. Swabia was an area which
formed part of modern Bavaria, Switzerland and Austria, and was
the centre of rule of the early Holy Roman Empire.]*

H.E. Count / Graf Brian Joseph Arundell of Wardour
(Count of The Holy Roman Empire)

H.E. Count / Graf William Arundell of Wardour
(Count of The Holy Roman Empire)

H.E. Countess / Graefin Janis LaRayne Hastings-Arundell of
Wardour
(Countess of The Holy Roman Empire)

H.E. Countess / Graefin Susan Jordan Howard Arundell of
Wardour
(Countess of The Holy Roman Empire)

BARCLAY de TOLLY
H.E. Count / Graf Rob Barclay de Tolly
Baron / Freiherr Barclay
(Count and Baron of The Holy Roman Empire)

BARON BAKER
H.E. Baron / Freiherr William Allen Baker
(Baron of The Holy Roman Empire)

LORDSHIPS OF THE MANOR OF BERRINGTON AND OF GRUNSTON
Part of the Patrimony of the Kingdom of Westphalia
(Lordship of The Holy Roman Empire)

[Author's observation: The kingdom of Westphalia is an area in the west of Germany which embraced the major cities of Dortmund, Münster and Osnabrück.]

BARON BECK
H.E. Baron / Freiherr Salvino A. Beck
Reichsritter of The Holy Roman Empire
(Baron of The Holy Roman Empire)

[Author's observation: Reichsritter *is a German word for the designation of an Imperial Knight.]*

BARON BENDELL
H.E. Baron / Freiherr James M. Bendell
Reichsritter of The Holy Roman Empire
(Baron of The Holy Roman Empire)

COUNT BENENDICT
H.E. Count / Graf Orlando Ivan Benendict
(Count and Baron of The Holy Roman Empire)

PRINCELY COUNT OF BENTINCK
H.M.Ill.H. Count / Graf Timothy Bentinck und Waldeck Limpurg, 12th Earl of Portland, Viscount Woodstock. Count of the Holy Roman Empire, for the Hon William Bentinck, Baron of the Duchy of Guelders, 2nd surviving son of Baron Hans Wilhelm Bentinck, 1st Earl of Portland, by Imperial Letters Patent of 29 December in the year 1732.
(Sovereign Princely Count of The Holy Roman Empire.)

H.Ill.H. Count / Graf William Jack Henry Bentinck und Waldeck
Limpurg, Viscount Woodstock
(Princely Count of The Holy Roman Empire)

H.Ill.H. Count / Graf Jasper James Mellowes Bentinck und
Waldeck Limpurg
(Princely Count of The Holy Roman Empire)

COUNT HARVEY OF BRISTOL
H.E. Count / Graf Simon John Harvey of Bristol
(Count of The Holy Roman Empire)

BARON BROWN
H.E. Baron / Freiherr Philip James Brown
(Baron of The Holy Roman Empire)

COUNT COBERLY
(See: Principality of Reichenberg)

BARON CARR
H.E. Baron / Freiherr John Joseph Carr
Reichsritter of The Holy Roman Empire
(Baron of The Holy Roman Empire)

BARON CREGAN
H.E. Baron / Freiherr William J. Cregan
Reichsritter of The Holy Roman Empire
(Baron of The Holy Roman Empire)

BARON COOPER
H.E. Baron / Freiherr Rufus Henry Cooper
(Baron of The Holy Roman Empire)

COUNT COSTELLO
H.E. Count / Graf Maxwell Costello
(Count of The Holy Roman Empire)

COUNT CLARK
H.E. Count / Graf Robert Clark
(Count in The Holy Roman Empire)

PRINCELY HOUSE OF COWPER
George Nassau Clavering Cowper, Earl Cowper was created on
31 January 1778 a Prince of The Holy Roman Empire, by the
Emperor Joseph II, he was Ambassador at Vienna, and his sister
was the mistress of the Emperor.
(Prince of The Holy Roman Empire)

BARON COX
H.E. Baron / Freiherr Rick Cox
Reichsritter of The Holy Roman Empire
(Baron of The Holy Roman Empire)

D'ALBYVILLE
H.E. Marquis d'Albyville. Grantee Sir Ignatius White, alias
d'Albyville, Sir Ignatius White was a 17th century diplomatist,
who was Ambassador at Brussels and afterwards at Madrid.
He followed James II to France at the Revolution.
(Marquis, Baron and Knight of The Holy Roman Empire)

BARON D'AGUILAR
Baron / Freiherr Ephraim Lópes Pereira d'Aguilar
(Baron of The Holy Roman Empire)

COUNT D'ALTON
Richard D'Alton is described as Lieutenant-General in the Imperial
Army and the title is said to have been conferred by the Empress
Maria Theresa. He seems to have been a haul type of soldier of
fortune who earned a reputation for carrying out harsh orders in a
brutal and unfeeling way. He distinguished himself in Transylvania
by using high gallows for hanging insurgents and when the Emperor
suppressed the old constitution of the Austrian Netherlands in 1789,

D'Alton was employed to crush the opposition. But the Flemings cornered him and his regulars in Brussels and forced him to surrender.

(Count of The Holy Roman Empire)

H.E. Count / Graf Michael D'Alton
(Count of the Holy Roman Empire)

H.E. Count / Graf Tomas Manning D'Alton
(Count of the Holy Roman Empire)

H.E. Count / Graf Jeffrey D'Alton
(Count of the Holy Roman Empire)

H.E. Count / Graf Tomas D'Alton
(Count of the Holy Roman Empire)

H.E. Count / Graf James D'Alton
(Count of the Holy Roman Empire)

H.E. Count / Graf Denis D'Alton
(Count of the Holy Roman Empire)

H.E. Count / Graf Benjamin D'Alton
(Count of the Holy Roman Empire)

H.E. Countess / Graefin Jennifer Buckland D'Alton
(Countess of the Holy Roman Empire)

H.E. Countess / Graefin Jennifer D'Alton
(Countess of the Holy Roman Empire)

H.E. Countess / Graefin Nicola D'Alton
(Countess of the Holy Roman Empire)

H.E. Countess / Graefin Anne Hede D'Alton
(Countess of the Holy Roman Empire)

H.E. Countess / Graefin Susan Belk D'Alton
(Countess of the Holy Roman Empire)

COUNT DE SALIS
H.E. Count / Graf John de Salis. Count of the Holy Roman
Empire, for Peter de Salis, by Imperial Letters Patent 12 March
1748, whose son Jerome, 2nd Count de Salis, had been naturalised
a British subject 24 March 1730, and whose descendant received a
Royal License for himself and his descendants 4 April 1809.
(Count of The Holy Roman Empire)

PRINCELY HOUSE OF DEVARAJ
H.S.H. Prince / Furst Sanjit Roshan Devaraj
(Prince of The Holy Roman Empire)

BARONY OF DROMCUMMER
Part of the Patrimony of the Kingdom of Westphalia
(Barony of The Holy Roman Empire)

BARON DILLON
Baron / Freiherr Dillon. Baron of the Holy Roman Empire, for
Festus O'Kelly, of Tycooly, to whom the remainder was granted
by Emperor Francis I, on 25th November 1767.
(Baron of The Holy Roman Empire)

BARON DUNN
H.E. Baron / Freiherr Rev. Raymond V. Dunn
Reichsritter of The Holy Roman Empire
(Baron of The Holy Roman Empire)

DUCAL HOUSE OF DUDLEY

Sir Robert Dudley, son of Queen Elizabeth's Earl of Leicester, who claimed the title, but failed to prove the marriage of his parents. He was a distinguished sailor, shipbuilder, a man of science and settled in Florence where he was employed by the Grand Duke of Tuscany after becoming a Roman Catholic. He was created Duke of Northumberland and Earl of Warwick under Imperial Letters of the Holy Roman Empire by the Emperor. His wife, whom he had deserted for another lady, was made a Duchess in the Grand Duchy of Tuscany.

(Duke and Earl of The Holy Roman Empire)

COUNT FORD

(See: Princely County of Oberstein)
H.Ill.H. Count / Graf Maxwell Charles Griffen Ford
Princely Count of Oberstein, Count and Baron Ford
(Princely Count and Baron of The Holy Roman Empire)

COUNT GRADY

(See: Princely Count of Uslar)
H.Ill.H. Count / Graf John von Uslar
Princely Count / Graf of Uslar
Count / Graf and Baron / Freiherr Grady
Reichsritter of The Holy Roman Empire
(Princely Count and Baron of The Holy Roman Empire)

COUNT GARLAND

(See: Count of Sohlingen)

COUNT GRANVILLE

Count of the Holy Roman Empire, created 27 January 1684.
Charles Granville, Viscount Lansdown, son of the Earl of Bath and grandson of Sir Bevil Granville, the hero of the battles of Stratton and Lansdown in the Civil War. He was given his

Countship of the Empire for distinguished services in the War against the Turks.
(Count of The Holy Roman Empire)

BARON GUY
H.E. Baron / Freiherr Glen Guy
(Baron of The Holy Roman Empire)

PRINCELY HOUSE OF HOFFMAN
H.S.H. Prince / Furst Michael von Heidelberg
Prince / Furst von Heidelberg
Count / Graf and Baron / Freiherr von Hoffman
(Prince, Count and Baron of The Holy Roman Empire)

BARON JACKMAN
H.E. Baron / Freiherr Graham Jackman
(Baron of The Holy Roman Empire)

COUNT JOHNSON
(See: Princely County of Eisenberg)

COUNT LAUTENS
H.E. Count / Graf Stephen Lautens
(Count of The Holy Roman Empire)

COUNT LESLIE
H.E. Count / Graf Leslie
Heirs of Walter Leslie, 2nd son of John Leslie, 10th Baron of Balquhain, 1606-1667.
(Count of the Holy Roman Empire)

COUNT LEWINS
H.E. Count / Graf Douglas Lewins
(Count of The Holy Roman Empire)

LE BLON
Sir John Le Blon, Knight of the Holy Roman Empire,
Title created on 5 April 1744.
(Knight of the Holy Roman Empire)

COUNT LOCKHART
Count Lockhart, Count of the Holy Roman Empire, created
25 March 1783 for James Lockhart Wishart. Belonged to the
Jacobite family of Lockhart of Carnwath. He served with the
Austrian Army in the Seven Years War.
(Count of The Holy Roman Empire)

COUNT LISLE
H.E. Count / Graf Hunter Wood Lisle
(Count in The Holy Roman Empire)

PRINCELY & DUCAL HOUSE OF MARLBOROUGH
H.S.H. John George Vanderbilt Henry Spencer-Churchill,
11th Duke of Marlborough, Prince / Furst of Mindleheim
(Prince of The Holy Roman Empire)

REICHSRITTER NAUMES
Monsignor Rev. Father Matthew Naumes
Prelate of Krak des Chevaliers
Reichsritter of The Holy Roman Empire
(Imperial Knight of The Holy Roman Empire)

COUNTESS McNEAL
H.E. Countess / Graefin Jenny Maria McNeal
(Countess of the Holy Roman Empire)

BARON MERCER
H.E. Baron / Freiherr Christopher John Mercer
(Baron of The Holy Roman Empire)

COUNT MULRY
H.E. Count / Graf John Mulry
(Count of the Holy Roman Empire)

DUCAL HOUSE OF MASSA AND CARRARA
H.S.H. Don John Malcolm James Cracknell
Duke and Marquis of Massa and Carrara
(Duke and Marquis of The Holy Roman Empire)

COUNT O'KELLY
H.E. Count / Graf William O'Kelly.
Count of the Holy Roman Empire for Festus O'Kelly of Tycooly
to whom the remainder was granted) by Emperor Francis I
on 25 November 1767.
(Count of The Holy Roman Empire)

H.E. Count / Graf Eoin O'Kelly
Count of the Holy Roman Empire for Festus O'Kelly of Tycooly
to whom the remainder was granted) by Emperor Francis I
on 25 November 1767.
(Count of The Holy Roman Empire)

BARON O'HARA
H.E. Baron / Freiherr Michael K. O'Hara
Reichsritter of The Holy Roman Empire
(Baron of The Holy Roman Empire)

COUNT KITCHENER
H.E. Count / Graf Albert Edward Kitchener
Count / Graf and Baron / Freiherr Kitchener
(Count and Baron of The Holy Roman Empire)

H.E. Countess / Graefin Winfred Rosa Emily Kitchener
(Countess and Baroness of The Holy Roman Empire)

COUNT O'DONELL

H.E. Count / Graf Heinrich O'Donell. Count of the Holy Roman Empire for O'Donell by Imperial Letters Patent of 11 November 1763, last known male, Heinrich Nikolaus Ferdinand Kolumban, Count O'Donell, b. 1908.
(Count of The Holy Roman Empire)

COUNT RUMFORD

H.E. Count / Graf Rumford. Count Rumford invented the Rumford fireplace.
He was born Benjamin Thompson in Woburn, Massachusetts, in 1753. Because he was a loyalist, he left (abruptly) with the British in 1776. He spent much of his life as an employee of the Bavarian Court.
(Count of The Holy Roman Empire)

COUNT SHIRLEY

H.E. Count / Graf Anthony Shirley, Count / Graf Shirley
   (Count of The Holy Roman Empire)

BARON SMITH

H.E. Baron / Freiherr Bernard J. Smith
Reichsritter of The Holy Roman Empire
(Baron of The Holy Roman Empire)

COUNT SPENCER

H.E. Count / Graf Gregory Stuart Boyd Spencer
Baron / Freiherr Boyd Spencer
(Count and Baron of The Holy Roman Empire)

COUNT ST. PAUL

Horace St. Paul, Count of the Holy Roman Empire. Conferred by Emperor Francis I in Vienna on 20 July 1759. The title was granted in recognition of Col. St. Paul's services during the Seven Years War. He was in the Austrian Army for 14 years. He was

born in London in 1729 and died at Ewart Park, Northumberland in 1812.
(Count of The Holy Roman Empire)

COUNT TAAFE
H.E. Count / Graf Edward Taafe, Viscount Taafe. Count of the Holy Roman Empire, for Nicholas Taafe, 6th Viscount Taafe – in the Peerage of Ireland; title suspended by the Crown as the then Viscount had taken up arms in the Imperial Austrian Armies, 1919 – was created a Count by Imperial Letters Patent of 30 September 1758.
(Count of The Holy Roman Empire)

BARON VAN OPPEN
H.E. Baron / Freiherr Eric van Oppen
Reichsritter of The Holy Roman Empire
(Baron of The Holy Roman Empire)

BARON WEGER
H.E. Baron / Freiherr Kenneth H. Weger
Reichsritter of The Holy Roman Empire
(Baron of The Holy Roman Empire)

BARON WOLFF
Charles Godfrey Wolff was created a Baron of the Holy Roman Empire on 16 February 1791 by the Emperor Leopold II under Imperial patent.
(Baron of The Holy Roman Empire)

COUNT YORK
H.E. Count / Graf Robert York
Count / Graf and Baron / Freiherr York
(Count and Baron of The Holy Roman Empire)

One of the closing lines states: 'For God, Germany and the Empire!'

In addition to the above, there is a further organisation known as the *Imperial and Royal Society of the Almanach de Chivalry*. The following is a list of the official members of this society as listed on its website: www.almanachdechivalry.com/index.html

His Holiness Pope Benedict XVI, Bishop of Rome
Supreme Primate of The Holy Roman Empire
(Prince of The Holy Roman Empire)

His Imperial and Royal Highness Prince Karl Friedrich of Germany

Duke of Swabia, Duke of Saxe-Altenburg
Prince of Schwarzburg-Sondershausen-Rudolstadt
(Prince of The Holy Roman Empire)

His Majesty King Juan Carlos I of Spain
(Prince of The Holy Roman Empire)

Her Majesty Queen Elizabeth II of the United Kingdom
of Great Britain and Northern Ireland
(Princess of The Holy Roman Empire)

Her Majesty Queen Margrethe II of Denmark
(Princess of The Holy Roman Empire)

Her Majesty Queen Beatrix of The Netherlands
(Princess of The Holy Roman Empire)

His Majesty Czar Simeon II of The Bulgarians
Prime Minister of Bulgaria
(Prince of The Holy Roman Empire)

His Majesty King Albert II of The Belgians
(Prince of The Holy Roman Empire)

His Majesty King Harald V of Norway
(Prince of The Holy Roman Empire)

His Majesty King Michael I of Romania
(Prince of The Holy Roman Empire)

His Majesty King Constantine II of Greece
(Prince of The Holy Roman Empire)

His Majesty King Carl XVI Gustaf of Sweden

His Royal Highness Grand Duke Henri of Luxembourg
(Prince of The Holy Roman Empire)

His Most Serene Highness Prince Hans-Adam II of Liechtenstein
(Prince of The Holy Roman Empire)

His Most Serene Highness Prince Albert II of Monaco

Her Imperial Highness Grand Duchess Maria of Russia
(Princess of The Holy Roman Empire)

His Imperial Highness Grand Duke George of Russia
(Prince of The Holy Roman Empire)

His Royal Highness Prince Vittorio Emanuele of Savoy,
The Prince of Naples
(Prince of The Holy Roman Empire)

His Imperial and Royal Highness Prince Dom Pedro Orleans-
Bragança

His Imperial and Royal Highness The Archduke Otto von
Habsburg of Austria
(Prince of The Holy Roman Empire)

His Imperial and Royal Highness The Archduke Sigismund
of Austria
Prince of Tuscany
(Prince of The Holy Roman Empire)

His Imperial and Royal Highness Prince George Friedrich
of Prussia
(Prince of The Holy Roman Empire)

His Royal Highness Margrave Max of Baden
(Margrave of The Holy Roman Empire)

[Author's observation: The term Margrave *is deemed to be an
equivalent of* Marquess.*]*

His Royal Highness Duke Franz of Bavaria
(Prince of The Holy Roman Empire)

His Royal Highness Prince Wilhelm Albert Raphael Maria
of Urach
Count of Württemberg, 5th Duke of Urach, *de jure* King
of Lithuania
(Duke of The Holy Roman Empire)

His Royal Highness Margrave Maria Emanuel of Meissen
(Margrave of The Holy Roman Empire)

His Royal Highness Prince Michael of Saxe-Weimar-Eisenach
(Prince of The Holy Roman Empire)

His Royal Highness Duke Friedrich-Konrad of Saxe-Meiningen
(Duke of The Holy Roman Empire)

His Highness Duke Borwin of Mecklenburg-Strelitz
(Duke of The Holy Roman Empire)

His Highness Duke Eduard of Anhalt
(Duke of The Holy Roman Empire)

His Highness Duke Andreas of Saxe-Coburg and Gotha
(Duke of The Holy Roman Empire)

His Most Serene Highness Prince Jean-Engelbert of Arenberg
(Prince of The Holy Roman Empire)

His Serene Highness Prince York of Schaumburg-Lippe
(Prince of The Holy Roman Empire)

His Serene Highness Prince Stefan-Johannes von Regensburg
Furst von Regensburg, Frieherr von Aachen
(Prince and Baron of The Holy Roman Empire)

His Illustrious Highness Count Ernst Leonhard von Harrach
zu Rohrau und Thannhausen
(Princely Count of The Holy Roman Empire)

His Most Illustrious Highness Count Charles von Giech
(Count of The Holy Roman Empire)

His Excellency Count Frederick Wilhelm von Buren
(Count of The Holy Roman Empire)

His Excellency Count Leopold zu Limpurg und Gaildorf
(Count of The Holy Roman Empire)

His Excellency Baron Christian Wilhelm von Groditz
(Baron of The Holy Roman Empire)

Under a section headed *The History of the Almanach de Chivalry*, it states the following, recorded verbatim as follows:

> *The Almanach de Chivalry, was formally founded on Christmas day 2002, by His Imperial and Royal Highness Prince Karl Friedrich of Germany, Duke of Swabia, Duke of Saxe-Altenburg, de jure Emperor Charles VIII I.R., by Imperial decree, to promote the cause of Christian Chivalry and to list by Almanach the various Imperial, Royal and Princely Orders of Knighthood in Europe and Christendom… and hopes you will be able to have a better understanding of Chivalry in its Universal Glory. The formal rise of Chivalry brought with it messages of loyalty, heroism, glory and brotherly love. It was seized upon by the Sovereigns and Princes of Europe, who saw it as the ideal stratagem with which to bond men of rank and military expertise, creating elite brotherhoods of Chivalric Orders that would serve them in both war and peace.*

Also included within the *Almanach de Chivalry* is a list of the prominent Orders of Knighthood across Europe. Two lists which are worth noting are as follows, again recorded word for word as displayed:

The Papal Orders of the Holy See of Saint Peter

The Order of Christ

This rarely given distinction cannot strictly be characterized today as an Order of Knighthood, but more as an award of honour of the highest possible standing. The recent reforms of the Papal Orders by Pope Paul VI, the Order of Christ was reserved to Catholic Heads of State to whom it might be given only to commemorate very special occasions at which the Pope himself was present. This Order was last awarded in 1987 to the late Frà Angelo de Mojana, 77th Prince and Grand Master of the Sovereign Military Order of Malta on the occasion of the twenty-fifth anniversary of his election to the Grand Magistery; he died the following year. With the recent death of King Baudouin of the Belgians there are no living Knights of the Papal Supreme Order of Christ and there is a considered opinion that the present Pope may have decided to let it fall into abeyance, at least for the present.

The Order of The Golden Spur
(Ordo Militia Aurata or Ordine dello Speron d'Oro o Milizia Aurata) Cannot be dated for certain but is referred to as being conferred under Pope Paul III in 1539. 1 class: Knight.

The Order of Pius
(Ordo Pianus or Ordine Piano) Established by Pope Pius IX 17.6.1847. 4 classes, the 3rd class being divided into 2 degrees: Grand Collar, Grand Cross, Commander with Star/Commander, Knight.

The Order of St Gregory the Great
The Papal Order of Saint Gregory was originally founded by Pope Gregory XVI on 1 September 1831, in four classes – Knights Grand Cross (1st class), Knights Grand Cross (2nd class), Knights Commander, and Knights. The regulations concerning the grades and uniform were then expanded in a further Bull dated 30 May 1834. As part of the reform of the Papal Orders instituted by Saint Pius X on 7 February 1905, the grades of the Order were modified by the addition of a Star for a higher category of Knights Commander and the suppression of the 2nd class of Knight Grand Cross, paralleling the grades of the Ordine Piano and the newly founded Order of Saint Sylvester. Pius X also assigned to the Papal Knights a particular place in Papal processions and in ceremonies of the Church. Awards of the Order are usually made on the recommendation of Diocesan Bishops or Nuncios for specific services. Unlike membership of the Military Orders (Malta, the Holy Sepulchre), membership of the Order of Saint Gregory does not impose any special obligations. It is thus the preferred award to acknowledge an individual's particular meritorious service to the Church. A Bishop wishing to recommend an individual for this

honour will a draw up a suitable letter proposing the candidates name, with a c.v., and forward it with his recommendation to the Apostolic Nuncio. The Nuncio may consult with the Bishop regarding the grade – if, perhaps, the grade suggested may be inappropriate – but will then usually forward the recommendation to the Secretariat of State. There the candidate's name is considered carefully and, if approved, a Diploma is drawn up in Latin (and the candidates forenames are translated into Latin) and this receives the signature and seal of the Cardinal Secretary of State. It is then delivered to the recipient. Usually, Papal awards give rise to a nominal "tax" charge to cover the expenses concerned – this charge may be paid by the Diocese but is usually reimbursed by the recipient. The highest rank, that of Grand Cross, is an exceptional award – less than eight US citizens have received this honour in the past twenty-two years – and those who receive it have usually already been a member of Saint Gregory in one of the lower ranks before being promoted. Knights Grand Cross wear a more elaborate uniform with more extensive silver braid, a white plumed hat instead of the black plumes common to the lower ranks, while the badge is worn from the broad Riband of the Order on the left hip and the breast star. Knights Commander wear a less elaborate uniform, with the badge worn suspended from the ribbon of the Order around the neck, while the higher rank (Knight Commander with Star) also wears the breast star. There have only been twenty-two awards of the senior rank of Commander with Star since 1974 to US citizens. Knights wear a simpler uniform without the braid on the collar and sleeves, with the badge worn from a ribbon suspended on the left breast. Since 1994 Dames have been admitted in the same grades as men. They do not wear the uniform or sword, their Grand Cross Riband is narrower and the Commander's badge is worn from a bow on the left breast.

The Order of St. Silvester
(Ordo Sanctus Silvestri Papae or Ordine di San Silvestro Papa)
Established by Pope Gregory XVI 31.10.1841.
The Order has 3 classes, the 2nd class being divided into two degrees:
Grand Cross, Commander with Star/Commander, Knight.

The Order of The Holy Sepulchre of Jerusalem
Founded: 24 January 1868 (revival)
Protecting Authority: The Holy See
Ribbon : Black (Order of the Cross of Merit: White and red;
The Palms of Jerusalem: Black)
Grand Master: His Eminence Carlo Cardinal Furno.

The Papal Lateran Cross
(Crux Lateranum or Croce Lateranese) Established by Pope Leo
XIII 18.2.1903.
The order has 3 degrees: gold, silver, bronze.

The Cross of Honour
'Pro Ecclesia et Pontifice' (Cruz or Croce 'Pro Ecclesia et
Pontifice')
Established by Pope Leo XIII 17.7.1888.

The second list is as follows, again recorded word for word:

The Imperial and Royal Orders of the Holy Roman Empire of the
German Nation

The Imperial and Royal Orders of Knighthood held under The
Supreme Protection of The Imperial and Royal Electoral House
of Germany

The Imperial Order of the Teutonic Knights of St. Mary's
Hospital in Jerusalem
(2 Classes, Limited 1190 Knights)
Grand Master: H.I.&.R.H. Prince Karl Friedrich von
Deutschland
de jure Emperor Charles VIII of Germany

The Imperial and Royal Augustinian Order of The White Eagle
of The Holy Roman Empire
(1 Class) Grand Master: H.I.&.R.H.
Prince Karl Friedrich von Deutschland , de jure Emperor Charles
VIII of Germany

The Imperial Carinthian Order of Karl Der Grosse
Grand Master: H.I.&.R.H. Prince Karl Friedrich
von Deutschland
de jure Emperor Charles VIII of Germany
(1 Class)

The Imperial and Royal Order of St. Hubert of Lorraine
(1 Class) Grand Master: H.I.&.R.H. Prince Karl Friedrich
von Deutschland
de jure Emperor Charles VIII of Germany

The German Order of the Hospital of St. John of Jerusalem
Grand Priory of Germany
Imperial Johanniter Order (4 Classes)
Protecting Authority: H.I.&.R.H. Prince Karl Friedrich
of Germany
Ribbon : Black. Head Styled Grand Prior

The Imperial and Royal Order of St. George of Carinthia
(1 Class) Grand Master: H.I.&.R.H. Prince Karl Friedrich
von Deutschland
de jure Emperor Charles VIII of Germany

The Imperial and Royal Military Order of St. Henry
Grand Master: H.I.&.R.H. Prince Karl Friedrich von Deutschland
de jure Emperor Charles VIII of Germany
(2 Classes)

The Order of The Slaves of Virtue
Grand Master: H.I.&.R.H. Prince Karl Friedrich von Deutschland
de jure Emperor Charles VIII of Germany
(1 Class)

The Imperial Order of the Ancient Nobility
of the Four Emperors (1 Class)
Grand Master: H.I.&.R.H. Prince Karl Friedrich von Deutschland
de jure Emperor Charles VIII of German.

The Imperial Order of the Defeated Dragon
Grand Master: H.I.&.R.H. Prince Karl Friedrich von Deutschland
de jure Emperor Charles VIII of Germany
(2 Classes)

The Imperial Order of St. Rupert of Salzburg
Grand Master: H.I.&.R.H. Prince Karl Friedrich von Deutschland
de jure Emperor Charles VIII of Germany
(1 Class)

The Royal Order of the Eagle of Este (1 Class)
Grand Master: H.I.&.R.H. Princess Maria of Germany

The Royal Order of St. Elizabeth (1 Class)
Grand Master: H.I.&.R.H. Princess Maria of Germany

The Order of St. Michael (1 Class)
Grand Master: H.I.&.R.H. Prince Karl Friedrich von Deutschland
de jure Emperor Charles VIII of Germany

Noting that the *Almanach* was established in 2002, it again reinforces the prospect that aspirations for the re-establishment of the Holy Roman Empire are alive and well.

Bibliography and references

Aachen and its Cathedral by Alfred Carl – Einhard (2005)

Birth of Europe, The by Jacques le Goff

Cambridge Illustrated History of the Middle Ages edited by Robert Fossier

Catholic Encyclopaedia

Charlemagne by Roger Collins

Chivalry by Malcolm Keen – Yale University Press

Chronicle of the Popes, The by P.G. Maxwell Stuart

Crown and Nobility by Anthony Tuck

Early Middle Ages, The by Rosamond McKitterick

Emperor Charlemagne, The by Russell Chamberlin – Sutton Publishing (2004)

Encyclopaedia Britannica

Encyclopaedia of Religion (2nd Edition)

First Crusade, The by Thomas Asbridge

Formation of Christendom, The by Judith Herrin

Friars, The by Kenneth W. Rowlands

Greatest Knight, The by Elizabeth Chadwick

Hiram Key, The by Christopher Knight and Robert Lomas

History of Pagan Europe, The by Prudence Jones and Nigel Pennick

History of the County of Warwick

History of the County of Wiltshire

History of the Knights Templar by Charles G. Addison (first published 1842)

History of the Most Noble Order of the Garter and Several Orders of Knighthood in Europe by Elias Ashmole (rare book held in Sussex Library Archives, 1672)

Holy Blood and the Holy Grail, The by Michael Baigent, Richard Leigh and Henry Lincoln – Arrow Books (1996)

Holy Kingdom, The by Adrian Gilbert with Alan Wilson and Baram Blackett

Hospitallers – The History of the Order of St John by Jonathan Riley-Smith – Hambledon Press (1999)

Hutcheson Encyclopaedia

Keepers of the Kingdom – The Ancient Offices of Britain by Alistair Bruce, Julian Calder and Mark Cator – Wiedenfeld and Nicolson (2000)

Knights Templar Chronology, The by George Smart – AuthorHouse (2005)

Knights Templar in Britain, The by Evelyn Lord

Knights Templar Revealed by Alan Butler and Stephen Dafoe – Constable and Robinson (2006)

L'Age D'or des Ecoles de Chartres by Edouard Jeanuneau – Houvet Chartres (2000)

Salisbury Miscellany (A) by David Hollian – Sutton Publishing

Templars, The by Malcolm Barber and Keith Bate – Manchester University Press (2002)

Templars, The by Piers Paul Read – Wiedenfeld and Nicolson (1999)

Temple Church – A History in Pictures by Robin Griffith-Jones Master of the Temple (2008)

Temple Manor by S.E. Rigold – English Heritage (1962)

Trial of the Templars, The by Malcom Barber – Cambridge University Press (2006)

Warriors and Bankers, The by Alan Butler and Stephen Dafoe – Lewis Masonic (2006)

William Marshall, Knighthood, War and Chivalry by David Crouch

William Marshall: The Flower of Chivalry by Georges Duby

Yellow Cross, The by René Weis – Penguin Books (2001)

Notes

Section 2
Days before the Knight

1   Elias Ashmole – *History of the Most Noble Order of the Garter and Several other Orders of Knighthood in Europe*

2   Wikipedia –Celeres

3   Wikipedia – Tullius

4   Elias Ashmole – *History of the Most Noble Order of the Garter*, quoting Dionysus

5   Elias Ashmole – *History of the Most Noble Order of the Garter*

6   Elias Ashmole – *History of the Most Noble Order of the Garter*

7   Elias Ashmole – *History of the Most Noble Order of the Garter*

8   Catholic Encyclopedia – Jesus

9   Catholic Encyclopedia – Messiah

10   Catholic Encyclopedia

11   Catholic Encyclopedia – Christ

12   Catholic Encyclopedia

13   Catholic Encyclopedia

14   Catholic Encyclopedia

15   Catholic Encyclopedia

16   *The Holy Kingdom* by Adrian Gilbert, with Alan Wilson and Baram Blackett

17   Catholic Encyclopedia

18   *The Emperor Charlemagne* by Russell Chamberlin

19   *The Emperor Charlemagne* by Russell Chamberlin

20   Catholic Encyclopedia – New Advent – States of the Church

21   Catholic Encyclopedia – New Advent – States of the Church

22   *The Emperor Charlemagne* by Russell Chamberlin – Epilogue

23   *The Holy Kingdom* by Adrian Gilbert

24   Wikipedia – King Arthur

25   Noted from information on display in the Great Hall, Winchester

Section 3
The Making of Kings, Nobles and Knights

26   Catholic Encyclopedia

27   Catholic Encyclopedia – Simony

28   Elias Ashmole – *The History of the Most Noble Order of the Garter and Several other Orders of Knighthood in Europe* – The Black Eagle

29   *Chivalry* by Maurice Keen – Yale University Press, p78

30   Catholic Encyclopedia

31   There are various versions of the making of a knight, although the rituals involved were very similar. In some instances, for example, the colour of the garments changes; the dubbing process is not the laying of the sword on either shoulder, but touching the top of the head to symbolise wisdom in judgements; or simply placing the sword across outstretched hands. The example used in the text is a modified version of that indicated in works referencing the poem *Ordene of Chevalerie*; the relating of a tale involving Hugh, Count of Tiberias and Saladin, wherein Hugh, as a prisoner of Saladin, takes Saladin through the ritual of Christian knighthood, as noted in the Introduction of Maurice Keen's book *Chivalry*

32   Encyclopaedia Britannica – Charles IV

33   *Chivalry* by Maurice Keen – Yale University Press, chapter IV

34   Catholic Encyclopedia – Pope Urban II

Section 4
The Major Orders of Knighthood

35   As indicated in *The History of the Most Noble Order of the Garter and Several other Orders of Knighthood* – Elias Ashmole

36   From the website of the Equestrian Order of the Holy Sepulchre at http://www.khs.org.uk/index.htm

37   *The History of the Most Noble Order of the Garter and Several other Orders of Knighthood* – Elias Ashmole

38   *The History of the Most Noble Order of the Garter and Several other Orders of Knighthood* – Elias Ashmole

39   Catholic Encyclopedia

40   *The spelling of Godfroi varies depending on the source referred to. According to genealogists, his full name and title was Duke Gottfried IV of Lower Lorraine, and the son of Count of Boulogne.*

41   *The Holy Blood and the Holy Grail* by Baigent, Leigh and Lincoln, Arrow Books, chapter 3

42   Catholic Encyclopedia

43   *The Knights Templar Chronology* by George Smart

44   *The Hiram Key* by Robert Lomas and Christopher Knight

45   James Orchard Halliwell – *Early History of Freemasonry in England*, 1840

46   *The Trial of the Templars* by Malcolm Barber, Cambridge University Press, page 223 (reprinted 2006)

47   See *Early History of Freemasonry in England*, James Orchard Halliwell

48   See *The Yellow Cross, the story of the last Cathars*, Rene Wiess, 2000;
      also *The Holy Blood and the Holy Grail*, Baigent, Leigh and Lincoln

49   Copied verbatim from the Vatican website -
      http://asv.vatican.va/en/doc/1308.htm

50   BBC website in 2009 – http://news.bbc.co.uk/1/hi/magazine/7050713.stm

51   *The History of the Most Noble Order of the Garter and Several other Orders of
      Knighthood* – Elias Ashmole

52   As per text at http://www.chivalricorders.org/vatican/teutonic.htm

53.   http://www.royal.gov.uk/MonarchUK/Honours/
      OrderoftheGarter.aspx

54   Wikipedia – *Honi soit qui mal y pense*

55   *The History of the Most Noble Order of the Garter and Several other Orders of
      Knighthood* – Elias Ashmole, chapter V

56   *The History of the Most Noble Order of the Garter and Several other Orders of
      Knighthood* – Elias Ashmole, chapter V

57   *The History of the Most Noble Order of the Garter and Several other Orders of
      Knighthood* – Elias Ashmole, chapter IV

58   *The History of the Most Noble Order of the Garter and Several other Orders of
      Knighthood* – Elias Ashmole, chapter VII

59   *The History of the Most Noble Order of the Garter and Several other Orders of
      Knighthood* – Elias Ashmole, chapter VII

60   *The History of the Most Noble Order of the Garter and Several other Orders of
      Knighthood* – Elias Ashmole, chapter IV

61   *The History of the Most Noble Order of the Garter and Several other Orders of
      Knighthood* – Elias Ashmole, chapter IV

62   *The History of the Most Noble Order of the Garter and Several other Orders of
      Knighthood* – Elias Ashmole, chapter IV

63   *The History of the Most Noble Order of the Garter and Several other Orders of
      Knighthood* – Elias Ashmole, chapter IV

64   *The History of the Most Noble Order of the Garter and Several other Orders of
      Knighthood* – Elias Ashmole, chapter IV

65   Catholic Encyclopedia – St George

66   Catholic Encyclopedia – St George

67   Catholic Encyclopedia – St Andrew

68   *The History of the Most Noble Order of the Garter and Several other Orders of
      Knighthood* – Elias Ashmole – The Order of the Golden Fleece

69   Glasgow University, section on Arts and Emblems, French Emblems,
      quoting Claude Paradine at
      http://www.emblems.arts.gla.ac.uk/french/emblem.php?id=FPAa024

70   Noted during a visit to City Hall, Bruges

71   *The History of the Most Noble Order of the Garter and Several other Orders of
      Knighthood* – Elias Ashmole – The Order of Amaranta

72   *Christina Queen of Sweden* by F. W. Baix BA, W.H. Allen and Co, London, 1890; electronic version The University of Connecticut Libraries

73   Based on information contained in UK government material on the British monarchy, a version of which can be viewed at: http://www.royal.gov.uk/MonarchUK/Honours/OrderofStPatrick.aspx

Section 5
Symbolism and the Knights

74   Catholic Encyclopedia – Holy Sepulchre
75   Catholic Encyclopedia – Holy Sepulchre

Section 6
Prominent Knights of Old

76   *A Salisbury Miscellany* by David Hilliam – Sutton Publishing

77   Attributed to William Dodworth – *An historical account of the Episcopal see, and cathedral of Sarum or Salisbury*, and restated on www.wikipedia.org.uk/William_II_Longespee

78   Catholic Encyclopedia – St Leonard

79.   Notes by the Reverend Dr Anthony Carr, Minister of the church, as provided by Wroxall Abbey Estate

Index

A

B

C

D

E

F

G

H

J

K

L

M

N

O